TWENTIETH CENTURY INTERPRETATIONS
OF

THE BEGGAR'S OPERA

A Collection of Critical Essays

Edited by
YVONNE NOBLE

Prentice-Hall, Inc. A SPECTRUM BOOK *Englewood Cliffs, N.J.*

Library of Congress Cataloging in Publication Data

NOBLE, YVONNE, COMP.
  Twentieth century interpretations of The beggar's opera.

  (Twentieth century interpretations) (A Spectrum Book)
  Bibliography: p.
  1. Gay, John, 1685–1732. The beggar's opera. I. Title.
II. Title: The beggar's opera.
PR3473.B6N6   822'.5   74–31464
ISBN 0-13-069815-6
ISBN 0-13-069807-5 pbk.

The excerpt from Goldoni's *Memoirs* (1814), I, 185–86, as quoted by M. F. Robinson in "The Aria in Opera Seria, 1725–1780," *RMA Proceedings*, 1961–62 is used by kind permission of the Royal Musical Association, London.

10 9 8 7 6 5 4 3 2

PRENTICE-HALL INTERNATIONAL, INC. (*London*)
PRENTICE-HALL OF AUSTRALIA, PTY. LTD. (*Sydney*)
PRENTICE-HALL OF CANADA, LTD. (*Toronto*)
PRENTICE-HALL OF INDIA PRIVATE LIMITED (*New Delhi*)
PRENTICE-HALL OF JAPAN, INC. (*Tokyo*)

Contents

Introduction:
The Beggar's Opera in Its Own Time

by Yvonne Noble

I

On January 29, 1728, there opened in London one of the most remarkably successful—and one of the most original—pieces in the history of English theater: *The Beggar's Opera*. It burst into history. In ways unmatched by other works of literature, its existence constitutes an Event. It attained a popularity in its first seasons so widespread and so sustained that even careful Pope could call it "unprecedented, and almost incredible." It was a palpable force politically, stinging the Prime Minister, Robert Walpole, so sharply that he banned Gay's sequel, *Polly*, from production, and emboldening other playwrights of the Opposition to a flood of outspoken criticism that Walpole dammed only by enacting in 1737 a repressive Licensing Act. It changed the course of music, by helping turn Handel away from operas to oratorios and by standing ancestor to Mozart's comic operas, to Gilbert and Sullivan's operettas, and to American musical comedy. It originated a genre, ballad opera (a play abounding with songs set to familiar tunes), of which dozens appeared in the next few decades, though not one nearly such a masterpiece as Gay's first. It goes on in our time inspiring adaptations and imitations, among them another masterpiece, Brecht and Weill's *The Threepenny Opera*. And in itself *The Beggar's Opera* quickly claimed a place among the handful of plays (other than Shakespeare's) that are standards in the English repertoire, that go on being revived year after year, century after century, through all shifts in taste and cultural outlook, constantly delighting their audiences.

Its author, John Gay, was a versatile and able poet whose accomplishment has unfortunately been overshadowed in modern eyes by that of Pope and Swift, who were his lifelong friends. Although his work was often drawn by the gravity of their more powerful minds toward the satiric irony they found most congenial, his own distinctive talent was quite different—truly comic in attitude and blessed with the essential light touch that the comic spirit requires; it flourished best just where Pope and Swift could not follow, in genres like drama and balladry, where the sense of community is important. Gay's songs are among the best lyrics for music in the language. As the author of fables, he has no peer in English. His plays range widely, from verse tragedy through pastoral,

1

comedy, farce, and the delightful "tragi-comi-pastoral farce" entitled *The What D'Ye Call It,* to our ballad operas and (so we believe) the text of what some find Handel's most satisfying opera, the pastoral *Acis and Galatea.* Humorless people have trouble in understanding that great ability lies behind literature of these unsolemn sorts; we find Gay, alive and dead, dogged by critics who attribute the best parts of his work to somebody else, or, as by repeating the old chestnut that *The Beggar's Opera* originated in Swift's idea of a "Newgate pastoral," imply that he had to get his ideas from somebody else. If we look unblinkered, however, at the canon of Gay's writings, we can see plainly that he was entirely capable of doing his own work, that he understood the nature of his special talents perfectly well, and that he was willing to follow those talents into unprecedented forms if they seemed likely to find their best exercise there. Of his many earlier works that contributed to the form of *The Beggar's Opera,* the burlesques of 1714–16—*The Shepherd's Week,* a burlesque eclogue; *Trivia; or, the Art of Walking the Streets of London,* a burlesque georgic; and *The What D'Ye Call It*—particularly deserve mention as manifestations of Gay's particular talent at work. Each begins as a literary burlesque, measuring the intentionally rarefied characters of the high literary form it invokes against the inelegant low equivalents it actually depicts. But so much vigor and good nature does Gay give his rustics, or Londoners, that in him the literary measurement becomes reciprocal: it begins to dignify the characters in the face of the form they inhabit. And finally, because of his affection for his characters, his interest in their customs and in the small details of their worlds, his indulgence toward their clumsy efforts at play- or eclogue-making, the emphasis of these burlesques gradually turns away from the mocking imitation of a form outside to the celebration of a world within; the pieces come to live on their own, shining with good humor. As he writes in the "Preface" to *The What D'Ye Call It*:

> . . . the sentiments of Princes and clowns have not in reality that difference which they seem to have: their thoughts are almost the same, and they only differ as the same thought is attended with a meanness or pomp of diction, or receive a different light from the circumstances each Character is conversant with.

Over a decade later, Gay reached back to these burlesques as he searched his earlier work for the elements, however disparate, that had in some way called out his truest talent, in order to fuse them together into the inspired new form that represents the culmination of his career. But while the essential elements of the form of *The Beggar's Opera* may have long stood potential in his writing, it required a cluster of public events in the London of the mid-1720's to make the matter that called them forth. With Gay we must now turn to look upon the London of his time.

II

John Gay was born in 1685 in a country town, Barnstaple in Devon, from which he came as a young man to London to serve as apprentice to a mercer. The city suited him, though commerce did not, and rather quickly we find him in the life he followed till he died, companion of statesmen, courtiers, and wits. His closest friends throughout his life were Pope and Swift, as I have mentioned, and the Duke and Duchess of Queensberry. For Gay's circle these years, however, were by no means consistently serene. Early in their friendship, during the latter years of Queen Anne, Gay and his literary friends (calling themselves the Scriblerus Club) shared a small and lofty circle with the Tory ministers Oxford and Bolingbroke, the men actually governing the country. The confidence the poets felt in this happy situation, particularly in their awareness of *being heard,* released in them a flow of creativity to which we are indebted for, among other works, *Gulliver's Travels, The Dunciad,* and *The Beggar's Opera* itself. The latter three pieces, however, were not worked out for over a decade (*Gulliver* was published in October 1726, *The Beggar's Opera* opened in January 1728, *The Dunciad* appeared the following May), and much of their meaning was shaped by the writers' altered circumstances and the altered tenor of the nation's political life in those subsequent years.

To its members, the Scriblerus Club's ostensible union of political power with literary preoccupations—intelligence, grace, elegance, life enacted and evaluated in moral terms and with the expectation of moral consistency—must have seemed a return of the Golden Age: had not literary men urged since the Greeks that the role of Poets was to instruct Princes? But they were realists enough to know that such felicity was not likely to last, and it did not. After Queen Anne's death in 1714, in came the Elector of Hanover—a man who was generally uninterested in England, its people, laws, customs, language, or arts—to be King of the country, and, not very long after, in came Robert Walpole as First Minister, to govern the country for what turned out to be, for the members of Gay's circle, the rest of their lives.

Walpole was gifted. He is celebrated by historians for creating the position of Prime Minister and for identifying its authority with the House of Commons (rather than the Lords). He is celebrated for securing the stable succession of the House of Hanover to the English throne and for keeping England, despite the second George's perpetual yearnings for military fame, out of entanglement in continental wars for a crucial quarter-century: his policies let the country outlive the disruptive, often bloody, factionalism that had characterized the seventeenth century and helped it to attain the settled conditions that enabled it to assume for a century and a half the empire of the seas. As John Loftis points out later in this book, our assessment of what matters in history is determined by our retrospective view, and Walpole has the unassailable substance of a leader who has been successful.

Walpole's solid accomplishments had not become manifest by the time of Gay's death in 1732; besides, while we moderns weigh them as accomplishments largely because they moved history towards what we find familiar, for the corresponding reason Gay and his friends deplored them. Walpole's first move was to break the chief Tory leaders so that there could be no future threat to the control of government by his own party, the Whigs. This he managed by playing on the general fear among English Protestants, far the largest religious group, that a Stuart Roman Catholic Monarchy might be restored. Oxford, accordingly, was held in the Tower for two years on a charge of treason before he emerged, acquitted but broken in spirit; Bolingbroke evaded a like fate only by fleeing to France; Swift, his hopes for a clerical preferment in England obliterated, was consigned to permanent exile in Dublin; and Pope, always liable to the restrictive legislation laid against Roman Catholics, slipped away from London to a secluded life upriver in Twickenham. Year after year—until long after Gay was dead—they nourished the hope that the setback was only temporary. Yet as the years wore on, years during which, as we know now, a new society—oligarchical, urban, commercial, and industrial—was taking shape, they were forced to watch the England they had known, with its familiar values, institutions, customs, and allegiances, steadily giving way to what seemed in their gloomier moods a base marketplace where shysters and hacks and grotesque foreigners swarmed.

All this time, too, they were confronted with the distressing spectacle of Walpole as the head of their government. However impressive we may find the skillful politician's understanding of how to grasp power and how to use it to accomplish material ends, most of us—especially those of us who feel powerless—long for our leaders to ennoble our lives, to be not only successful but statesmanly, to be wiser, more honorable, more dignified, more scrupulous, more cultivated than we, to foster what is valuable and to put down what is wicked. Walpole did not concern himself with such ideals. He was conversationally coarse, in later life physically gross (280 pounds), and considerably a self-aggrandizer, who built for himself during his time in office, with what money one may guess, an immense mansion back in Norfolk. Not for nothing was he called "the Great Man." The control his position gave him over the realm's elaborate system of patronage assured him a constant majority in Parliament. Beyond that, he saw nothing objectionable in distributing places to his close and then to his distant relations.

The Tory writers, who at one time had liked to imagine that their London might become the heart of a great civilization like Caesar Augustus's Rome, were dismayed by Walpole's schemes of bribery and nepotism, and also by his open contempt for all writing that was not political journalism. Gay was particularly galled. Less tough-minded than his friends, he had hoped that his poetry would earn him Court favor and hence patronage, and he allowed himself to go on entertaining this hope long after it was sensible to do so. His work is streaked with petitions, from his "Epistle to a Lady," the Princess of Wales, in 1714, through his *Fables* of 1727, dedicated to her son the young Duke of Cumberland and explicitly comparing their author to a Hare whose "friends" shift him off with excuses when he asks for help. Finally, after thirteen years of hinting, Gay's longed-for place was announced in October 1727 in the post-Coronation Household List of th· "Lady," who was now Queen Caroline: it was appointment to be Gen eman Usher to the two-year-old Princess Louisa, at £150 a year. However the gesture was intended (still a matter of debate) and whoever was responsible, Gay was badly disappointed and felt obliged to refuse the post ("So now all my expectations are vanish'd; and I have no prospect, but in depending wholly upon my self, and my own conduct"), and Swift made no bones about blaming Walpole. This release from concern against offending the Court must have sharpened the political satire in Gay's new work, already in draft, which depicted a modern, quite un-Augustan London, where Poets are no more than Beggars.

III

Even from the time *The Beggar's Opera* began to take shape, it inevitably assimilated a strong political coloration. In 1725 ingbroke had slipped back to England, offering a rallying point to a hose who, for whatever reason, opposed the King and his Minister. he Opposition recognized that their only hope lay in Walpole's fall. C dently expecting this to happen when the King died (for his heir ested Walpole near v as keenly as he detested his father), they set about preparing the public with satirical portraits of the Prime Minister. Their dismay was intense when Walpole did not fall, when, after only ten days' uncertainty following George I's death in June 1727, Walpole was restored to power. How fresh those days were in the public's mind can be seen from the subject of Peachum and Lockit's conversation in Act III, Scene V, "the Coronation account"—a phrase that to contemporary ears smacked of Walpole's scandalously great recent expenditures on the election and of the large amounts of public money set aside for the new monarch's use. *The Beggar's Opera* had been begun when Opposition hopes were high, and Gay had thought it amusing to incorporate into it some of the familiar Opposition jibes about "Statesmen," "Great Men," and "Robber(t)s." The jests at this level (including the satiric portraits of Walpole that audiences could discern in the characters of Macheath and Peachum) were what caused the political excitement during that first season—the public whom the Opposition had been coaching enjoyed its chance to laugh, and of course the Opposition themselves, having been plunged into gloom by the late events, seized upon Gay's unexpected success to preen up their spirits. The work's actual political strength, however, is much less superficial and partisan; it lies in the very moral nature of its comedy and burlesque.

Gay had early perceived the satiric possibilities in a comparison that the Opposition papers had made between Walpole and Jonathan Wild, a notorious criminal hanged in 1725. Wild had organized criminal London into his own empire: he licensed the thieves and pickpockets into gangs and assigned them strictly to districts or occasions (such as Court gatherings or services at St. Paul's Cathedral); he had warehouses for the receipt of stolen goods, artificers to alter goods so as to remove the identifying marks, and his own ship to carry them, if necessary, abroad for sale. His transactions he recorded in his books in multiple entry. He kept his felons in line by turning rebels in to the authorities ("peaching" them), for which he would receive the appropriate fixed reward (£40 for housebreaking and other graver crimes, if the man was convicted); to foster his image as a friend of the Law, he took to carrying a silver-headed staff which, he said, signified his position as "Thief-Taker General of Great Britain and Ireland."

Wild was clever in manipulating the law as it might apply to himself. Indeed, he built up his power in the first place by devising a way to circumvent a difficulty that thieves had run into in disposing of their goods because of a new law that made receiving a felony: he worked out a scheme simply to return stolen goods to the owner "as a public service" and for an unsolicited cash donation "in recognition of his contribution to justice." Those who failed to give, of course, found their property soon disappearing irrecoverably. A further value of the scheme was that it made many more things, such as personal papers and tradesmen's shopbooks, worth stealing. By 1718 so notorious had these practices become that Parliament was obliged to enact a statute specifically against them. Even so, Wild was able to continue unchecked for another seven years— because the public were happy to conspire with his duplicity. He had offices near the Courts, took retaining fees, and otherwise in word and manner compared his services to a lawyer's. He was finally arrested in quite a different connection—for provoking a brawl—and was hanged only when he went so far as to return some stolen lace to its owner by his own hand in his prison cell at Newgate.

In his professional practices Gay's Peachum reincarnates Wild without exaggeration. This would have been plain to early audiences immediately in Act I from Peachum's appearance, ledgers, and words, which include Wild's familiar comparison, "A Lawyer is an honest employment, so is mine." Gay's wit lies in bringing out the more submerged likenesses between Wild and Walpole—their success at attaining and retaining command over their societies; their brazenness; their duplicity; their bland materialism ("All these men have their price," we remember Walpole saying; Wild notes in his accounts, "One man, hanged, £40"); and, alas, their manipulation and corruption of a willing public. The superficial joke in lines like "the Statesman, because he's so great,/Thinks his trade as honest as mine" turns on our certainty that we know the difference between a criminal and a head of state. But one need not explore very far below the surface to strike Gay's fundamental vein: that there may in fact be no difference, other than in our unexamined habit of mind. A further complexity in this evaluation is represented by Peachum's own attitude, for *his* joke turns on the notion that statesmen are plainly inferior. The political force of Gay's comparison, carried out to such length, lies in its clear indictment of the leader who cares for nothing but the material, the commercial, and the expedient, both by showing us such a man in the figure of Peachum and by reminding us over and over that the Peachums flourish in the example of, and in the moral climate set by, the Court, the aristocracy, the First Minister—leaders of the society at large. When those in power are not better than we but worse, how far has corruption spread!

The emblem of Walpole's new society, as Maynard Mack observes, is the figure of Peachum. For him, men are merely "goods." They may be allowed to go on living for what profit one can make from their activity (one's "interest"), or they may be turned in for a flat cash payment. Those who do not think as toughly as he become his victims; ideals like loyalty, decency, honor, kindliness, love, become weaknesses, and he can make real fetters out of such "illusions." Among animals, as he sees it, preying upon one another is the natural way, and naturally the weak and encumbered must perish. Several excellent critics have seen the action of *The Beggar's Opera* as a conflict between bourgeois values, represented by the Peachums, and aristocratic ones, represented by Macheath—two ways of social *independence,* to take up Empson's term. I prefer to think of the conflict as between Peachum's system and *dependence,* what Gay implies when Polly says in Air 12 that her life, too, "depends" upon the rope that hangs her dear Macheath. In one term of the metaphor, she is killing him more quickly by adding her dead weight to his; this is true in the plot, too, for it is because of her that Peachum sets after Macheath. But audiences have always responded to Polly, especially, we are told, when she sings this very song; they recognize that what she stands for are the intangibles of mind and spirit that cannot exist without the protection of those who can move effectively within the system of a Peachum and yet see a goodness beyond self-interest. Perhaps it is fair to extend the intangibles Polly stands for to those of Art as well, to argue that she stands for the other heroines in the romances she reads, whose stylized speech and habits of mind she echoes ("O how I fear! how I tremble!" "Shall thy Polly hear from thee?").

The nature of the opposition between what Peachum stands for and what Polly stands for can be seen in the alternative endings of the *Opera.* Peachum's ending, the one that will endorse the terms of Walpole's world, the ending in which Macheath dies, is the "real" ending, the one that accurately reflects the world we live in. The other ending, the one that rescues Macheath (and so saves Polly as well), is shown to be just a fiction, "the kind of ending you get in a play," though, of course, it is "real" in the important sense of being the one the audience actually sees. Gay has enlisted all our affection for Macheath and Polly to serve in his indictment of Walpole, in whose world they must inevitably perish, and he makes an impressive demonstration of the power of art by showing that it can successfully combat the strength of a Peachum or a Walpole's single-mindedness both by creating and by saving them. I must not leave discussion of the ending, though, without admitting the ultimate irony: while art, in the form of *Gay*'s Opera, triumphs over Walpole's reality, this is done at the expense of the *Beggar*'s Opera, the artistic integrity of which he sells out for "the Taste of the Town." "Strict poetical Justice," like courtroom justice, would have hanged Macheath. Perhaps Walpole's system is the final conquerer after all, if even the Beggars and Poets cannot stand apart from the corruption.

IV

The Augustans were no less aware than we that England's historic strength in the world of Art lay in its literature, in that art which uniquely commands the intellectual, as well as the spiritual, moral, emotional, and aesthetic apprehensions. The Hanoverian court, on the other hand, whose first George could not even speak the English language fluently, cared little for literature, its members patronizing instead the art they preferred, Italian opera. The greatest contemporary composer of such opera was their own court musician, Handel, who had been theirs long before any of them saw England. At this time the form of Italian opera was dictated by a vast number of conventions (that this particular sort of aria be followed by that particular sort; that each singer immediately leave the stage after singing an aria; that the principal singers never open, but always close the acts; that the action be tragic but the ending comic; and so on through dozens), which, though at first glance seem the devisings of a madman, had actually evolved to display as brilliantly as possible an extraordinarily splendid sort of sound. We cannot recapture it: it is founded upon the unusual vocal capacities of rigorously trained *castrati.* Such ruthless subordination of every other aspect of the drama—sense, motivation, even bare intelligibility—seemed to literary men truly decadent—as hideous a perversion of the drama's moral purpose as the *castrato*'s physical disfiguration was of the body's. Inevitably Italian opera came to serve for the satirists as an exemplary instance of all that was "outlandish" and "unnatural" in their age.

One must admit that there was never any danger that this importation would take permanent root in English soil; even while Handel's Company was consolidating its international pre-eminence by obtaining a third of Europe's greatest singers, English audiences were growing weary of the unintelligibility and expense. They diverted themselves by making a vogue of the inevitable rivalry between prima donnas—between the new Faustina and the established Cuzzoni. They turned performances into contests of hissing and clapping between opposing claques. These goings-on reached their climax in June 1727, when the two prima donnas were provoked into engaging in a scuffle onstage. The Company closed prematurely that season and remained closed for a year before the transplantation of Italian opera was tried again.

It was just at the time when Italian opera was beginning to take on this raucous aspect that Gay would have been looking for a likely project to follow his *Fables*. One can easily see how the notion of burlesquing Italian opera would have appealed to him, and how attractive would have been the prospect of exercising again his gift for burlesque, together with his knack for plotting, swift characterization, and lively, speakable dialogue and the lyric talent that had made his ballads such lasting favorites. The details to fill out the notion must have come flooding in from his earlier experiences: the setting could be that local, contemporary, and inelegant London that had served him so well in his georgic burlesque *Trivia*; there the prison would simply be Newgate, and the heroic kings and queens London's rogues and whores. He could motivate the conventional plot reversal by means of a frame like the one he had used in his farce *The What D'Ye Call It*; furthermore, a hugely pregnant heroine like the one in that play would make the quarrel scene between his prima donnas even funnier; funnier yet, let the *castrato* be the father of her child; still better, let him be an amorous gallant. There must be arias in plenty, and a good number of them made up on similes, like Handel's— for the similes he could use the animals he had just been working with in the *Fables*; for the music he could simply use tunes everybody knew, the ones they sang at home and in the taverns and liked to hear at the theaters or from street-singers and rustic itinerants like Bowzybeus in *The Shepherd's Week*.

To savor this burlesque of Italian opera fully, we must pause to consider the distinction between the Beggar's Opera and Gay's. The former has the satiric properties of mock-heroic, that is, its irony cuts as much against the Beggar's stupefying failure to grasp the purpose of his medium —the creation of splendid music—as against the moral idiocy of Italian libretti (when judged from the literary point of view). We must presume that the Beggar has chosen to write an opera because he admires something about the originals, if only their vogue among the fashionable and influential. He is pleased to be able to offer James Chanter and Moll Lay something right up to date for their wedding entertainment. And so he naturalizes the Italian opera into his own community, keeping what seems familiar (prisons, poison, the turmoil of rival loves), abandoning what seems incomprehensible (the artful music, the Italian language, the recitative, the *castrati*), and making the rest out of the material of his world (there must be a Hero, so he undertakes to celebrate the hero of his people, the Highwayman). The Beggar's innocence of everything pertaining to the mode and purpose of high heroic art represents precisely the charm—and the limitation—of primitive art in any medium.

The Beggar is an artist, for his work is marked by his persistence in trying to make sense out of the conventions he adopts, not only in the ways I have mentioned, but by, for example, extending the flora and fauna in his similes from the swallows and larks that were felt to be "poetic" enough for kings and queens to sparrows, rats, chickens, wilting flowers, and contraband vessels—terms that seem to him appropriate for his characters to use in their efforts to make their meanings plain. We may approve his choosing sense over style and at the same time acknowledge that he blunders in handling the special decorum of the mode he wishes to follow, as he does again in his ending, which flows directly out of his plot and offers strong "poetical Justice," yet is nevertheless not the kind of ending an opera must have. The Beggar's moral concern as an artist serves as a judgment upon the Italian librettists whose work has abandoned such concern. That the Beggar is made into a bad artist, one who dismisses the moral integrity of his work for fashion, or mindless convention, or commercial success (as he has in the first place, for the same reasons, abandoned his native medium, the English play "with prologue and epilogue") further illustrates the corrupting influence of the librettists' practice, itself (we are meant to see) only an instance of the widespread corruption in the age generally.

The Beggar's Opera is shorter than Gay's by the extent of the frame on either end; it is a failure, for it has only one ending, which is ruined at the occasion of performance; and it is a slave to its model, a mere parody. In contrast, Gay's Opera dominates the model, for our attention is always fixed squarely upon his own characters and not upon whom they may be mimicking. He speedily establishes the Italian opera as part of his context by his title, by the Beggar's remarks in the "Introduction," and by the event of the Overture; thereafter, he can rely upon the notion of opera being kept at hand by the running device of the characters' bursting into song, so that he may draw upon its conventions and characteristics or ignore them, as he finds convenient. Accordingly, we understand that he chooses Macheath for his hero, and uses ballad tunes for his arias, not because, like the Beggar, he has failed to grasp the decorum of Italian opera, or because by their incongruity they might make the originals seem ridiculous, but because they are most suitable to his own internal purpose. Yet he draws in enough of the conventions to seem to have outmatched the Italian librettists on their own terms: the hackneyed similes are made lively and witty; the betrayals, poison, and prisons are made appropriate and plausible; and especially, by his device of the frame, the compulsory happy ending is at last justified.

Gay's attainment goes further. In the latter part of the previous century there had stirred in the playhouse what might have been the beginnings of English opera, had not its development been set back by the premature death of its most talented composer, Henry Purcell, and then extinguished entirely when Handel arrived with his pre-empting foreign genius. The English experiments had been, we might say, *playwright's* operas—literate, well-motivated plays with spoken dialogue, graced with the added embellishment of song. From the critical debates during the years before English opera succumbed in its contest with the Italian, we know that English opera, had it reached fulfillment, would have had English subject matter and English music and would have been performed in English by a native English cast. In an important sense, Gay's opera (a quarter-century later) is exactly these things—a playwright's opera with a vigorous English subject, performed in English by a native cast, and sung to native music. Here lies its strongest rejoinder to the "outlandish" art form and to all those who preferred it to the neglect of art of native growth.

V

In the widest sense, viewing the opposition of art forms as symbolic of the opposition of the whole cultures they imply, Gay's artistic triumph was only one of several aspects of *The Beggar's Opera* that invited audiences to reaffirm their allegiance to the native tradition. Some of the others are worth casting a glance at.

There are sixty-nine tunes in *The Beggar's Opera*, a staggering number for a single work, and one can hardly overestimate their influence on its tone. Gay selected his tunes from the canon that everyone knew—old ballads like "The Children in the Wood" and "Chevy Chase," the drinking songs and bawdy songs that Fielding's Squire Western liked, pastoral songs that girls like Sophia Western sang in their drawing rooms, long-lasting dance tunes, one or two airs of Handel's and Purcell's that had caught on outside the opera house, even a couple of his own ballads that had taken the mainstream, "All in the Downs" and " 'Twas when the seas were roaring." Their cumulative effect, therefore, was to elicit in the audience a deep sense of community—partly by their testimony to the culture that all Englishmen, of whatever class or occupation, have in common, "by heart"; partly by their happy evocation of companies of men and women singing and dancing at fairs, in taverns, at harvest festivals, at holiday parties, or laughing and applauding entertainers at theater or in the London streets; partly by their immediate power to induce the solidarity that comes from an audience's recognizing together a

shared norm and then the incongruities of deviation from that norm—
some twist, let us say, that Gay might be making in the passing tune's old
text or context. This circle of community extended, one is inclined to
think, to Gay's characters as well, for, as the Beggar might remind us,
these self-same songs were as much a part of their culture as of anyone's;
indeed, perhaps a more active part of their culture than of the average
man's, for, as I shall illustrate shortly, Gay's contexts frequently suggest
that the characters may be exercising a deliberate rhetorical attention in
selecting tunes to reinforce the sentiments they wish to convey. Hence the
songs serve powerfully to mitigate the divisive effect of Gay's satiric treatment of English society. Even though our understanding is deepened by
observing, with John Loftis, that "the effectiveness of the play depends
on the distance [Gay] establishes between the moral and social orders of
the dramatic action and those of the lives of his contemporaries," we
must bear in mind simultaneously that the music works to bridge that
distance. Even Peachum, and Walpole, and Wild are redeemed by this
circle of song.

The point I am making is that *The Beggar's Opera* exists in the comic
mode; that the satire, extensive and important as it is, alert as we should
be to its nuances, is throughout and finally encompassed by the values of
comedy. Thus, for example, while from the ironic perspective we may
attend to the psychological significance of what Empson has so discern-
ingly called to our attention—the characters' preoccupation with hanging, particularly when speaking of the gestures of love—still we must
remember that the prevailing comic tone operates always to drain from
the notion of death its horror and agony. That there simply cannot be
death for these characters the dynamics of the action repeatedly makes
manifest, most gloriously in its final spectacle, the celebration of Macheath's reprieve and triumph.

Macheath's context, too, contains traditions that register him on our
minds as a "comic" hero and therefore, I am persuaded, endorse him,
however much moralists and admirers of generations of Polly Peachums
may demur. One of these traditions is evoked through Gay's references
to tunes long associated with verses of bawdry and dalliance, largely of
the sort that conjure up successions of farmers' daughters exchanging
double-entendre and carnal favors with tinkers and other such casual
passers-by. In songs of this sort the singers' approval is given to those
who engage sexually with gusto. The continual presence of such tunes
in *The Beggar's Opera* argues strongly to the audience, with the compell-
ing logic of association, in favor of Macheath's amorous generosity over
the unkindly restraint implied in Polly's self-conscious innocence. Restraint and innocence are not admired in the tradition to which these
tunes belong, and Gay can hardly have been oblivious of this. Consider
Air 15, to choose one example out of dozens: Macheath, whom we are

seeing for the first time, is at last alone with his Polly and he character-
izes himself in a pretty compliment to her:

> My heart was so free,
> It rov'd like the Bee,
> 'Till *Polly* my passion requited;
> I sipt each flower,
> I chang'd ev'ry hour,
> But here ev'ry flower is united.

Superficially the song appears to imply that Macheath has accepted the
imperative of perpetual faithfulness to Polly, and it is surely in this sense
that she takes its meaning. But we should not join those who accuse
Macheath of having prevaricated in this song when later, at last entirely
alone with us and able to speak candidly, he confides that "Polly is most
confoundedly bit.—I love the sex. And a man who loves money, might
as well be contented with one guinea, as I with one woman" (II.iii).
Macheath in fact has made himself plain from the time of his first moment onstage, and not least in this very song. For while its words are
complimenting Polly, its tune is calling up (for everyone in the audience
who knew popular song) earlier and more familiar words, which make the
compliment conditional on her sexual compliance, and which tellingly
point out the crucial difference between public and private reality, between what one says and what one does:

> Come Fair one be kind, you never shall find,
> A Fellow so fit for a Lover;
> The World shall view my Passion for you,
> But never your Passion discover:
>
> I still will Complain of Frowns and Disdain,
> Tho' I revel thro' all your Charms;
> The World shall declare, I dye with Despair,
> When only I die in your Arms:
>
> I still will adore, Love more and more,
> But by *Jove* if you chance to prove Cruel,
> I'll get me a Miss, that freely will Kiss,
> Tho' after I drink Water-gruel.

This song was widely known through repeated appearances in a standard
backroom songbook, *Wit and Mirth, or Pills to Purge Melancholy.* Some
in Gay's audience might still recall its original context in Farquhar's
The Recruiting Officer (1706), where it was sung by another engaging
theatrical "Captain" and gallant, the eponymous hero, Captain Plume.
Every aspect of the tune's associations thus reinforces a true characterization of Macheath and at the same time identifies his attitude toward
life with others we have approved and enjoyed.

The character of Macheath is also validated in the *Opera* by the claims of "the Natural." If we return to the words Gay has written for Macheath in the song just quoted and gloss them against those given to Polly in Air 6 (*"Virgins* are like the fair flower in its lustre . . . Near it the Bees *in play* flutter and cluster. . . ."), we see that to ask Macheath to remain faithful to Polly is to ask him to leave Nature's usages for feigning and sterility. Can one doubt that it is best to be Macheath, vibrant and polyphiloprogenitive, in a world where most are life-denying, even death-dealing? Surely not, when we call to mind that in actual operatic performance Macheath's counterpart in Italian opera, the *castrato* as hero, would be continuously before the mind. The contrast Gay offers is thus too urgent, too fundamental, to allow grounds for hesitation—far better to be like one of the heathen, like "a Turk, with his doxies around," far better to be the lowly bee passing from flower to flower in Nature's true economy, than to honor an art that requires denial of life.

In sum, in Macheath—vigorous, English, generous, and manly—*The Beggar's Opera* implicitly appeals to its audiences to reaffirm their allegiance to what is native, natural, life-giving, and good—in short, to the values that in literature we generally call comic. In 1728, personal and political nostalgia would associate these values with the days, now mellow in memory, of Stuart and Tory rule, and it was this aspect of the work, when energized through public performance, that gave the *Opera* its exceptional importance outside the theater. Many men had felt uneasy because of what was happening to England under Walpole; *The Beggar's Opera* lifted their hearts, stirred their national pride, and, by its creation of community, emboldened them to testify—first in laughter, then in speech and print—against Walpole and the times. We, too, in the twentieth century, often find ourselves disheartened by what happens to our heritage or by leaders who we feel debase us; like our fellows two hundred and fifty years ago, we warm to Gay's genius still.

The Beggar's Opera: Mock-Pastoral
as the Cult of Independence

by William Empson

I

Some queer forces often at work in literature can be seen [in *The Beggar's Opera*] unusually clearly; its casualness and inclusiveness allow it to collect into it things that had been floating in tradition. It is both mock-heroic and mock-pastoral, but these take Heroic and Pastoral for granted; they must be used as conventions and so as ways of feeling if they are even to be denied. It would be as reasonable to say that human nature is exalted as that it is debased by this process; it makes Macheath seem like the heroes and swains no less than the heroes and swains like Macheath. If the joke against him is that he is vain to adopt the grand manner of the genteel rakes he at least stands their own final test; he has the courage to sustain it: "What would you have me say, ladies? You see this affair will soon be at an end, without my disobliging either of you." Indeed the audience did not want to despise heroic and pastoral but to enjoy them without feeling cheated; to turn them directly onto Marlborough and the contemporary ploughboy did make it feel cheated. The main joke is not against the characters of the play at all, nor does anyone in the discussions about its morality seem to have taken it as against the appalling penal code and prison system; it is against the important people who are *like* the characters; the main thing is the political attack and the principles behind it. But pastoral usually works like that; it describes the lives of "simple" low people to an audience of refined wealthy people, so as to make them think first "this is true about everyone" and then "this is specially true about us." So far as that goes the play is Swift's first conception of it—the pastoral method applied to Newgate.

There is a natural connection between heroic and pastoral before they are parodied, and this gives extra force to the comic mixture. Both when in their full form assume or preach what the parody need not laugh at,

Abridged from "The Beggar's Opera: *Mock-Pastoral as the Cult of Independence,*" *Chapter 6 of* Some Versions of Pastoral, *by William Empson (London: Chatto & Windus, 1935), pp. 195–250. First published in the United States as* English Pastoral Poetry *(New York: W. W. Norton & Company, Inc., 1938). Copyright © William Empson, 1935. All rights reserved. Abridged by permission of the author. Reprinted by permission of the author, Chatto & Windus Ltd., London, and New Directions Publishing Corporation, New York.*

a proper or beautiful relation between rich and poor. Hence they belong to the same play—they are the two stock halves of the double plot. . . .

One might think that the hearty relation between rich and poor which allowed of tricks between heroic and pastoral belonged mainly to the Elizabethans, and Gay surprisingly refers us back to them. The prologue to the *Opera* explains that it is a revival of the marriage masques, for the beggar artists (aristocrats no doubt in their own world) James Chanter and Moll Lay; the dance of prisoners in chains is a regular antimasque. Polly indeed views this dance simply as one of the charms of the world, but all its charms just then seem "an insult on my affliction," and the antimasque was a sort of symbolic insult. . . .

. . . Clearly it is important for a nation with a strong class-system to have an art-form that not merely evades but breaks through it, that makes the classes feel part of a larger unity or simply at home with each other. This may be done in odd ways, and as well by mockery as admiration. The half-conscious purpose behind the magical ideas of heroic and pastoral was being finely secured by the *Beggar's Opera* when the mob roared its applause both against and with the applause of Walpole.

One of the traditional ideas at the back of the hero was that he was half outside morality, because he must be half outside his tribe in order to mediate between it and God, or it and Nature. (In the same way the swain of pastoral is half Man half "natural." The corresponding idea in religion is that Christ is the scapegoat.) This in a queer way was still alive in the theatre; no perversion of human feeling might not be justified in the Restoration tragic hero, because he was so ideal, and the Restoration comic hero was a rogue because he was an aristocrat. The process of fixing these forms into conventions, the Tragedy of Admiration and the comedy of the predatory wit, undertaken because the forms had come to seem unreal, for some reason brought out their primitive ideas more sharply. Now on the one hand, this half-magical view seemed to the Augustans wicked as well as ridiculous; all men were men; they had just put down the witch-burnings; to a rational pacifism Marlborough and Alexander were bullies glorified by toadies. On the other hand, they were Tory poets, and the heroic tradition, always royalist (the king's divine right made the best magical symbol), had died on their hands. The only way to use the heroic convention was to turn it onto the mock-hero, the rogue, the man half-justified by pastoral, and the only romance to be extracted from the Whig government was to satirise it as the rogue. The two contradictory feelings were satisfied by the same attitude.

The rogue so conceived is not merely an object of satire; he is like the hero because he is strong enough to be independent of society (in some sense), and can therefore be the critic of it. There was a feeling that the unity of society had become somehow fishy—Hobbes' arguments in its favour, for instance, themselves products of civil war, only affected one the other way—and that the independent individual—the monad, the

gravitating particle—was now the only real unit. Hence the "rogue become judge" formula, with its obscure Christian connexions, is used by
a long series of writers for almost any purpose in hand. That is why the
merchant-pioneer Robinson Crusoe was such a hero and yet must apolo-
gise for his life. The interest of the Noble Savage (Dryden's phrase) was
that he was another myth about the politically and intellectually free
man. Macheath means laird of the open ground where he robs people; he
is king of the Waste Land. Dullness to Pope and Dryden is a goddess, so
that the theme of human folly is not trivial; she is a hideous danger to
civilisation; both she and the hero her representative can tell us with authority who is dull. Moll Flanders in her second robbery is tempted to
murder the child robbed, for greater safety; to escape from a moment of
horror at herself she becomes indignant with the child's parents, explains
how it ought to be looked after, and hopes the robbery will teach them
to take better care of it; this makes her touching and competent. All
Jonathan Wild's acts, according to himself in Fielding, might be excused
in a hero; a denunciation of heroes; it makes him intolerable. Gay has
many uses for the formula; a typical joke, that always delights a modern
audience, gives its application to marriage, when Peachum says on discovering the marriage of Polly:

> Married! the captain is a bold man, and will risk anything for money; to be
> sure he thinks her a fortune. Do you think your mother and I should have
> lived comfortably so long together if we had been married? Baggage!

The point of this is that it is a defence of marriage by one who thinks
he is attacking it; marriage is not exalted (one can accept the mockery
of the comedies), but it is more stable than its laws. The rogue has only
to free it from the offensive approval of society to find it natural.

It may be said that there is no real cult of independence in this, because the irony admits that the hero is not really independent or should
not be admired for it. Certainly the irony is necessary; later versions like
the raggle-taggle-gypsy business which merely admire the apparently free
man obviously leave out part of the truth. But though one may be puzzled
by what the *Opera* means, certainly the turns of phrase it uses are pro-
independent. The irony may well say that at a higher level the idea of
independence is all nonsense; everything is one, all men are dependent
on society, man can only be happy through generosity and a good conscience, or what not. But this does not annul the feeling for independence
because one is made to feel that at so high a level the common rules of
society are nonsense too. (This talk of levels seems evasive; the parallel
with extreme pacifism may make it less vague. Granted that it is true
that the right thing is for no man to resist another under any circumstances, a man who lives the life of a religious mendicant has or nearly
has the right to appeal to it. But a man who allows the police to protect
his property, however passively, is already not living by that rule and

cannot appeal to it, only to the lower-level idea of justice. Which level is being used is thus a matter of logical consistency.) The feeling of universality given by this ironical method is due to the reader's sense that "levels" are implied one above another. Not that this is the only way of giving a feeling of universality, which has been done, I suppose, more strongly by works whose thought and feeling seem straightforward, but it gives a clear case open to analysis. . . .

I should say then that the essential process behind the *Opera* was a resolution of heroic and pastoral into a cult of independence. But the word is capable of great shifts of meaning, chiefly because nobody can be independent altogether; Gay meant Peachum to be the villain, and there is a case for thinking him more independent than Macheath. The animus against him seems not only that due to a traitor; Gay dislikes him as a successful member of the shopkeeping middle class, whereas Macheath is either from a high class or a low one. . . .

II

The stock device of the play is a double irony like a Seidlitz powder, piling a dramatic irony onto what was already an irony. This forces one to read back a more complex irony onto the first one, and the composure of language of the characters makes us feel that the speaker took the whole sense for granted. So he is a pastoral character; he moves among fundamental truths. The trick of style that makes this plausible is Comic Primness, the double irony in the acceptance of a convention. This is never meant by the speaker as a single critical irony ("I pretend to agree with this only to make you use your judgment and see that it is wrong") —if an irony does that it does not seem prim—though the author may mean a critical irony when he assigns the character a primness. No sentence of the play is quite free from this trick; one might only doubt over "bring those villains to the gallows before you and I am satisfied," but though there is plain indignation in both Gay and Macheath, for Macheath to feel it is in a degree "rogue-become-judge," funny because self-righteous. One might divide Comic Primness with the usual divisions of comedy, according to the degree to which the inherent criticism is intended.

It may assume that the conventions are right and that to be good is to keep them; by applying them unexpectedly a sense of relief is put into their tightness, though one is still good; they are made to seem deliberately assumed, so that the normal man is unchanged beneath them, and this gives a sense of power and freedom just as custard-pie farce does. You may say that this simple type assumes the others—"What is an important truth for us would not be true on a higher level; it is good to see the superficiality of the rules we must none the less keep." But this may be inherent and yet well out of sight. This type goes with "free" comedy.

It may imply simply that the conventions are wrong, as a critical irony would, but if it is to remain Comic Primness it must then also imply that the speaker does not feel strong enough, or much desire, perhaps for selfish reasons, to stand up against them; he shelters behind them and feels cosy. One would use this in "critical" comedy, but it would be hard to make a complete critical comedy without ever leaving Comic Primness.

In full Comic Primness (an element of "full" comedy) the enjoyer gets the joke at both levels—both that which accepts and that which revolts against the convention that the speaker adopts primly. It is a play of judgment which implies not so much doubt as a full understanding of issues between which the enjoyer, with the humility of impertinence, does not propose to decide. For this pleasure of effective momentary simplification the arguments of the two sides must be pulling their weight on the ironist, and though he might be sincerely indignant if told so it is fair to call him conscious of them. A character who accepts this way of thinking tends to be forced into isolation by sheer strength of mind, and so into a philosophy of Independence.

This may be used for Ironical Humility, whose simplest gambit is to say, "I am not clever, educated, well born," or what not (as if you had a low standard to judge by), and then to imply that your standards are so high in the matter that the person you are humbling yourself before is quite out of sight. This has an amusing likeness to pastoral; the important man classes himself among low men, and the effect is to raise his standards, not to lower them. At the stage of "device prior to irony" this is an essential weapon of pastoral. I shall try to show that Polly uses it in this way. Also there is a feeling of ironical humility diffused generally through the play, as if the characters knew they were really much better than heroes and prime ministers, not merely like them, though they do not choose to say so clearly; the reason for this, I think, is that the pretence that Macheath and Walpole are both heroes is a sort of ironical humility in the author ("I am easily impressed"), not so much a critical one as one implying a reserve of force—"by this means I can understand them completely." Such an ironical humility is in effect like the attitude of the scientist; the observer must not alter what he observes but shrink to a mere eye. . . .

. . . This reserve about the degree to which one has got the matter in hand is of course a central method of irony. And the same effect may be given by someone who has not yet discovered that the problem exists; this may be called "genuine innocence" and in a way returns the third sort of Comic Primness to the first; the speaker feels that this is a lively way out, the hearer that it is rich in contradictions. This again may be imitated; the ironist may claim that to so good, natural, innocent, etc., a person as himself the problem in hand does not arise—what he says satisfies both parties to the dispute, almost like a pun; there is no way of proving that he is conscious of the problem—if he is made to hear of it he will still feel the same. This is best when so arranged that the other man cannot attempt to call the bluff without exposing himself, which arises naturally in the conventional setting of Comic Primness.

It is obvious that the characters of the *Opera* are in some sense "artificial," though to know just how impossible their talk is one would have to inspect the contemporary Newgate more thoroughly than Gay did or than we can do. (There is a story in *The Flying Post or Weekly Medley*, Jan. 11, 1728–9, to which attention has been drawn recently, showing Gay doing his best to get information from Peachum, but whether it is true or not makes no difference to the argument here.) This feeling of artificiality is, I think, given by the trick essential to mock-pastoral (or the dignity of style which allows of it); we are not enabled to know how much they and how much the author has put into their ironies. The puppets are plausible if they don't mean all that the play puts into their words and delightful if they do, and the shift between the two theories is so easy that we take them as both. One must add doubt about this to the previous doubts about such an irony in plain speech, with which it continually interlocks. To discuss "what the characters mean" is therefore a ridiculous occupation. I shall not, however, guard myself against this mistake; the trick would not work unless the audience was able to imagine for itself a level at which the meanings were just plausible and still delightful, and presumably the author does the same. It is clear, for instance, that Polly's remarks are arranged to fit in with a theory of innocence more than Macheath's, and his again more than Peachum's; Peachum would claim that the problem implied was irrelevant rather than unknown. Indeed the critical attack on "character" in plays previous to the stress on "personality" seems now often pedantic and beyond what a man like Mr. Eliot, who gave the attack its weight, would approve.

> *Filch.* Really, madam, I fear I shall be cut off in the flower of my youth, so that, every now and again, since I was pumped, I have thoughts of taking up and going to sea.

The *use* of Filch is that, when you meet young men in other walks of life taking themselves as seriously as he does, you can feel they are like him —unconscious in the way he is. On the other hand (so far as one can separate the feeling of a sentence from the feeling of the whole play), the author means no more by this than to keep up the joke of the style; he does not mean, for instance, that it is always stupid to take oneself seriously. I should call this the Free sort of Comic Primness in the author, and mere dignity in the speaker.

> *Mrs. Peachum.* You should go to Hockley-in-the-Hole, and to Marlebone, child, to learn valour; these are the schools that have bred so many great men. I thought, boy, by this time, thou hadst lost fear as well as shame. Poor lad! how little does he know yet of the Old Bailey! For the first fact, I'll ensure thee against being hanged; and going to sea, Filch, will come time

enough, upon a sentence of transportation. But now, since you have nothing better to do, even go to your book, and learn your catechism; for, really, a man makes but an ill figure in the ordinary's paper who cannot give a satisfactory answer to his questions.

"How little he knows yet of life!"—a simple twist localises each sentence to the sort of life considered. To localise so oddly is in itself to generalise —"One would find a prosing and complacent piety as the basis of feeling in any settled way of life." The main thing the author wants to say is "Take these as ordinary people; there is nothing queer about them but their economic conditions." Mrs. Peachum's kind of piety is indeed put in its place, but we are not told that it need be hypocritical. Yet there seems a touch of archness in "going to sea, Filch." One can only say that Mrs. Peachum is between simplicity and the first sort of Comic Primness, and the author between the first and the third.

> *Mrs. Peachum.* How the mother is to be pitied who hath handsome daughters! Locks, bolts, bars, and lectures of morality are nothing to them; they have as much pleasure in cheating a father and mother as in cheating at cards.

(This may look back to the first words of the divine Polly—to "make a poor hand of her beauty" would be not to cheat with her cards.) The surprise of the device of rhetoric by which Mrs. Peachum leaps from the instruments of her trade to a presumption of virtue makes us feel "all moral lectures are like locks; all used to imprison others as much as possible." By being a spirited and striking hypocrite she exposes a normal hypocrisy; the style makes the critic inherent in the rogue. How far she knows she is amusing for this reason is a more difficult question; I suppose she has the first sort of Comic Primness and the author the third.

> *Peachum.* A lazy dog. . . . This is death, without reprieve. I may venture to book him.

There is a conscious contrast between the decision and the prim caution about keeping the book neat.

> There is not a fellow that is cleverer in his way, and saves more goods out of the fire, than Ned.

He took advantage of the fire for robbery; "saving is a good act." Peachum's jokes may well be supposed to be unconscious from habit, but they imply "these ideas are a bit queer, and allow of latitude, but we have just as much right to them as the others." One must allow him the third sort of Comic Primness as well as his author, though the author's hatred of him brings in complications.

One cannot go far into the play without insisting on the distinction between the two sorts of rogues, which is made very clearly and gives a rich material for irony. The thieves and whores parody the aristocratic

ideal, the dishonest prison-keeper and thief-catcher and their families
parody the bourgeois ideal (though the divine Polly has a foot in both
camps); these two ideals are naturally at war, and the rise to power of
the bourgeois had made the war important. Their most obvious difference is in the form of Independence that they idealise; thus the Peachums'
chief objection to Macheath as a son-in-law is that he is a hanger-on of the
aristocracy.

> *Mrs. P.* Really, I am sorry, upon Polly's account, the captain hath not more
> discretion. What business hath he to keep company with lords and gentle-
> men? He should leave them to prey upon each other.
> *P.* Upon Polly's account? What the plague does the woman mean?

The discovery follows. The puzzle is that both Peachums feel dicing with
the aristocracy might involve independence in their sense as well as his.

> *Mrs. P.* I knew she was always a proud slut, and now the wench hath played
> the fool and married, because, forsooth, she would do like the gentry! Can
> you support the expense of a husband, hussy, in gaming, drinking, and
> whoring? . . . If you must be married, could you introduce nobody into
> our family but a highwayman? Why, thou foolish jade, thou wilt be as
> ill-used and as much neglected as if thou hadst married a lord.
> *P.* Let not your anger, my dear, break through the rules of decency; for the
> captain looks upon himself in the military capacity as a gentleman by his
> profession. Besides what he hath already, I know he is in a fair way of
> getting or dying, and both these, let me tell you, are most excellent chances
> for a wife. Tell me, hussy, are you ruined or no?
> *Mrs. P.* With Polly's fortune she might very well have gone off to a person of
> distinction; yes, that you might, you pouting slut.

Decency is the polite tone the bourgeois should keep up towards the
wasteful aristocrat he half despises, so it is not clear whether *ruined*
means "married" or "unmarried"; he is merely, with bourgeois primness,
getting the situation clear. But who is a *person of distinction?* Mrs.
Peachum is muddled enough to mean a real lord. (First joke; they will
marry anything for money.) But she may mean a wealthy merchant or
the squire he could become. (Second joke; this gets at the squires by
classing them as bourgeois and at the lords by preferring the squires.)
Squire Western, a generation later, was indignant in just this way at the
idea of marrying his daughter to a lord.

Gay forced this clash onto his material by splitting up the real Jonathan
Wild into Peachum and Macheath, who appear in the story as villain and
hero. Swift complained that Gay had wasted a chance of good mock-heroic
in Macheath's last speech to the gang; he should have said "let my empire
be to the worthiest" like Alexander. Gay was busy with his real feelings,
and Macheath says, "Bring those villains to the gallows before you, and
I am satisfied." But though he hates Peachum he makes him the parody
of a real sort of dignity, that of the man making an independent income

in his own line of business, and seems to have been puzzled between the two ideals in his own life. In the play the conflict is hardly made real except in the character of Polly; the fact that both parties are compared to Walpole serves to weaken it to the tone of comedy.

The ironies of the two parties are naturally of different intentions.

Jemmy. . . . Why are the laws levelled at us? Are we more dishonest than the rest of mankind? What we win, gentlemen, is our own, by the law of arms and the right of conquest.
[This specially heroic member peached.]
Crook. Where shall we find such another set of practical philosophers, who, to a man, are above the fear of death?
Wat. Sound men, and true.
Robin. Of tried courage, and indefatigable industry.
Ned. Who is there here that would not die for his friend?
Harry. Who is there here that would betray him for his interest?
Mat. Show me a gang of courtiers that can say as much.
Ben. We are for a just partition of the world, for every man hath a right to enjoy life.

The main effect of this mutual comparison, of the assumption of a heroic manner here, is to make the aristocrats seem wicked and the thieves vain. But even for this purpose it must act the other way, and make both charming by exchanging their virtues; that the aristocrats can be satirised like this partly justifies the thieves, and to extend to Walpole's government the sort of sympathy it was generous to feel for the thieves was strong satire precisely because it was gay. The author means the passage hardly less than the thieves do as a statement of an attitude admittedly heroic; Ben Budge anticipates Jefferson, and the whole complaint against the morality of the play was that they are too hard to answer. No doubt there is a further critical irony in the author—"the whole business of admiring Marlborough and Alexander is nonsense"; and in people like thieves, in whom heroism does so much less harm than politicians, Gay is ready enough for an irresponsible sort of admiration. It seems enough, if one requires a tidy formula, to say that the thieves have both grandeur and the first sort of Comic Primness and their author the third.

The political ironies of Peachum and Lockit are of a different sort. The difficulty in saying whether they mean their ironies does not arise because they are simple-minded but because they are indifferent; they bring out the justification that they are necessary to the state and partake of its dignity firmly and steadily, as a habitual politeness, and this goes on till we see them as portentous figures with the whole idea of the state, sometimes a cloud that's dragonish, dissolving in their hands.

Peachum. In one respect indeed we may be reckoned dishonest, because, like great statesmen, we encourage those who betray their friends.
Lockit. Such language, brother, anywhere else might turn to your prejudice. Learn to be more guarded, I beg you.

Either "it is not safe to accuse the great" or "it is bad for any man's credit to admit that in anything he is as bad as they are." But there is no sense of surprise in this double meaning; the primness of caution is merely indistinguishable from the primness of superior virtue.

> *Peachum.* 'Tis for our mutual interest, 'tis for the interest of the world that we should agree. If I said anything, brother, to the prejudice of your credit, I ask pardon.

Credit is used both about business and glory—"that fellow, though he were to live these six months, will never come to the gallows with any credit." *The world* may be the whole of society or Society, the only people who are "anybody," the rich who alone receive the benefits of civilisation. The traditional hero has a magical effect on everything; the Whig politicians act like tradesmen but affect the whole country; Lockit and Peachum have the heroic dignity of the great because they too have a calculating indifference to other men's lives. The point of the joke is that the villains are right, not that they are wrong; "the root of the normal order of society is a mean injustice; it is ludicrous to be complacent about this; but one cannot conceive its being otherwise." The conclusion is not that society should be altered but that only the individual can be admired.

This double-irony method, out of which the jokes are constructed, is inherent in the whole movement of the story. We feel that Macheath's death is not "downright deep tragedy," nor his reprieve—a sort of insult to the audience not made real in the world of the play—a happy ending, because, after all, the characters, from their extraordinary way of life, are all going to die soon anyway; then this turns back and we feel that we are all going to die soon anyway. One of the splendid plain phrases of Macheath brings out the feeling very sharply:

> A moment of time may make us unhappy for ever.

The antithesis might make *for ever* "in the life of eternity" from a speaker who expected such a thing, or as derived from heaven "in one of those moments whose value seems outside time." His life seems the more dazzlingly brief because "for ever" assumes it is unending.

> That Jemmy Twitcher should peach me I own surprised me. 'Tis a plain proof that the world is all alike, and that even our gang can no more trust one another than other people; therefore, I beg you, gentlemen, to look well to yourselves, for, in all probability, you may live some months longer.

"And no more; take care because you are in danger" is the plain sense; but the turn of the phrase suggests "You may live as long as several months, so it is worth taking trouble. If you were dying soon like me you might be at peace." It is by these faint double meanings that he gets genuine dignity out of his ironical and genteel calm.

An odd trick is used to drive this home; as most literature uses the idea of our eventual death as a sort of frame or test for its conception of happiness, so this play uses hanging.

> *Lucy.* How happy am I, if you say this from your heart! For I love thee so, that I could sooner bear to see thee hanged than in the arms of another.

It is true enough, but she means merely "dead" by *hanged;* no other form of death occurs to her.

> *Mrs. P.* Away, hussy. Hang your husband, and be dutiful.

Hang here has its real sense crossed with the light use in swearing— "don't trouble about him; he's a nuisance; be dutiful to your parents."

> *Polly.* And will absence change your love?
> *Mach.* If you doubt it, let me stay—and be hanged.

"Whatever happens" or even "and be hanged to you," but he really would be hanged.

> *Macheath* (in prison). To what a woeful plight have I brought myself! Here must I (all day long, till I am hanged) be confined to hear the reproaches of a wench who lays her ruin at my door.

His natural courage, and the joke that the scolding woman is a terror to which all others are as nothing, give "till I am hanged" the force of "for the rest of my life," as if he was merely married to her. Finally as a clear light use:

> *Peachum.* Come home, you slut, and when your fellow is hanged, hang yourself, to make your family some amends.

Hanging in the songs may even become a sort of covert metaphor for true love. "Oh twist thy fetters about me, that he may not haul me from thee," cries Polly very gracefully, but her song while her father is hauling carries a different suggestion.

> No power on earth can e'er divide
> The knot that sacred love hath tied.
> When parents draw against our mind
> The true love's knot they faster bind.

It is the hangman's knot, and the irony goes on echoing through the play. The songs can afford to be metaphysical poetry in spite of their date because they are intended to be comically "low"; only an age of reason could put so much beauty into burlesque or would feel it needed the protection; they take on the vigour of thought which does not fear to be absurd. This excellence depends on the same ironical generosity—

a feeling that life is fresh among these people—as lies behind Gay's whole attitude to his characters. (The point that genuine pastoral could then only be reached through burlesque was indeed made clearly by Johnson about Gay's own admirable *Pastorals*.)

There are two elements in the joke of this. One comes from the use of the local details of a special way of life for poetry regardless of how they seem to outsiders, like Johnson's *Rambler* showing how an Esquimaux would take metaphors for his love-rhetoric from seal-blubber. This in itself is satisfying to the age of reason because it shows the universal forces at work. Secondly it uses the connection between death (here hanging) and the sexual act, which is not merely a favourite of Freud but a common joke of the period; the first effect of this is to give an odd ironical courage to the wit of the characters.

> Here ends all dispute, for the rest of our lives,
> For this way, at once, I please all my wives.
> Which way shall I turn me, how can I decide?
> Wives, the day of our death, are as fond as a bride.

The joke need not be given the additional deathliness of the joke against marriage:

> *Mrs. Trapes.* If you have blacks of any kind, brought in of late, mantoes, velvet scarfs, petticoats, let it be what you will, I am your chap, for all my ladies are very fond of mourning.

Both the ladies want to be hanged "with" Macheath, in the supreme song of the play; "*but* hark," he replies, there is the bell; this is real death, which one dies alone.

A song by Mrs. Peachum, that lady of easy sentiment, introduced early to make us clear on the point, shows the range of ideas in this direct and casual comedy.

> If any wench Venus' girdle wear,
> Though she be never so ugly,
> Lilies and roses will quickly appear,
> And her face look wondrous smugly.

A rich irony identifies the beauty created by desire in the eye of the beholder with self-satisfaction. The last word admits and enjoys the banality of the preceding flower-symbols.

> Behind the left ear so fit but a cord
> (A rope so charming a zone is!)

Monks use them as zones; they stand for asceticism.

> The youth in his cart hath the air of a lord,

Macheath is a "captain"; it is the military hero's chariot of triumph. (When the cart is driven away he is left hanging.)

> And we cry, There dies an Adonis!
>
> —Whose annual wound in Lebanon allured
> The Syrian damsels to lament his fate
> In amorous ditties all a summer's day—

—Whose tragic sacrifice, every spring, like Christ, makes the crops grow. It is a rare case of the full use of the myth.

At Mrs. Peachum's first entry she finds her husband deciding which thief to hang next sessions; her cue is the end of the laugh at a string of aliases for Walpole.

> *Mrs. P.* What of Bob Booty, husband? I hope nothing bad hath betided him. You know, my dear, he's a favourite customer of mine—'twas he, made me a present of this ring.
>
> *P.* I have set his name down in the black list, that's all, my dear; he spends his life among women, and, as soon as his money is gone, one or other of the ladies will hang him for the reward, and there's forty pound lost to us for ever!
>
> *Mrs. P.* You know, my dear, I never meddle in matters of death; I always leave those affairs to you. Women, indeed, are bitter bad judges in these cases; for they are so partial to the brave, that they think every man handsome who is going to the camp, or the gallows.

The song follows. "Spends his life among women" means among prostitutes; not to say so implies that they are what all women are. Mrs. P.'s callous squeamishness only points the moral; the reason that all women are bitter bad judges about killing men by treachery is that they find so much interest in doing it to their lovers. It is the first hint of that eerie insistence on the sex war by which the play makes betrayal itself a lascivious act.

Perhaps the most grisly version of this notion is the one relapse into sentiment of the great Peachum. By this time Mrs. Peachum (who pleaded for a brave man before) is firmly entrenched in brutality behind her bourgeois "duty."

> *(Mrs. Peachum, Peachum, Polly listening.)*
>
> *Mrs. P.* The thing, husband, must and shall be done. For the sake of intelligence we must take other measures and have him peached the next session without her consent. If she will not know her duty we know ours.
>
> *P.* But, really, my dear! it grieves one's heart to take off a great man. When I consider his personal bravery, his fine stratagems, how much we have already got by him, and how much more we may get, methinks I can't find it in my heart to have a hand in his death: I wish you could have made Polly undertake it.
>
> *Mrs. P.* But in a case of necessity—our own lives are in danger.
>
> *P.* Then indeed we must comply with the customs of the world, and make gratitude give way to interest.

Then indeed—when not heroic one can always be sure to be respectable, because bourgeois, because self-seeking. She started with the insinuating pomp of the language of diplomacy. Their lives are in no danger; they only think Macheath will betray them because they think he is like Peachum. To be heroic would be to hang on for what they can get. Warmed into feelings of generosity by this situation, and fretfully wishing that Polly might save him the moral effect of deciding to violate them, he shows a fleeting sympathy with romantic love, which so often kills its loved one, and of which at other times, in his bourgeois virtue, he disapproves. Swift is beaten clean off the field here.

The same idea is implicit in one of the purest of Polly's fancies.

(*Lucy, Macheath, Polly.* [*The condemned Hold.*])
Polly (entering). Where is my dear husband? Was ever a rope intended for this neck! Oh, let me throw my arms about it, and throttle thee with love. . . . What means my love? not one kind word! not one kind look! Think what thy Polly suffers to see thee in this condition!

> Thus when the swallow, seeking prey,
>   Within the sash is closely pent,
> His consort with bemoaning lay
>   Without sits pining for the event.
> Her chattering lovers round her skim;
> She heeds them not, poor bird, her soul's with him.

Her first words say that her love is death; her love has caused his arrest; the presence of her love here only makes it impossible for him to be saved by the love of Lucy. "Think what your Polly suffers"; even without these accidents her love would be mere additional torture. And for what *event* is the consort (which also seeks *prey*) of this swallow *pining*? *Event* may mean "whatever happens," but the sense thrown at us is "the thing happening," the exciting thing; they both mean to be in at the death.

Lucy. Am I then bilked of my virtue?

"The thing I have *paid* for?"—the slang verb drags in a ludicrous and frightfully irrelevant bit of money-satire. Only the unyielding courage of Macheath, who keeps the thing firmly on the level of the obvious, gives one the strength to take it as comedy or even to feel the pathos of the appeal of Polly.

Lucy. Hadst thou been hanged five months ago, I had been happy.
Polly. And I too. If you had been kind to me till death, it would not have vexed me—and that's no very unreasonable request (though from a wife) to a man who hath not above seven or eight days to live.

He takes so completely for granted their state of self-centredness tempered by blood-lust that the main overtone of her speech is that so often important to the play—"we have all very few days to live, and must live with spirit." The selfishness of her remarks reconciles us to his selfish treatment of her, and the idea behind their pathos to his way of life.

So that to follow up the ideas of "love-betrayal-death," the sacred delight in the tragedy of the hero, is to reach those of "pathetic right to selfishness," the ideal of Independence. This comes out more clearly in the grand betrayal scene of the second act, of Macheath by the prostitutes. The climax is one of the double ironies.

> *Jenny.* These are the tools of a man of honour. Cards and dice are only fit for cowardly cheats, who prey on their friends.
> (She takes up the pistol; Tawdry takes up the other.)

(First laugh; the great are like the rogues but more despicable.) Having got his pistols she calls in the police. (Second laugh; the rogues are after all as despicable as the great.) But this is not merely a trick of surprise because she means it; "we are better than the others only because we know the truth about all human beings"; the characters are always making this generalisation. "Of all beasts of prey," remarks Lockit, "mankind is the only sociable one." The play only defends its characters by making them seem the norm of mankind and its most informed critics, and does this chiefly by the time-interval in their ironies.

> *Jenny.* I must and will have a kiss to give my wine a zest.
> (They take him about the neck, and make signs to the constables, who rush in upon him.)
> *Peachum.* I seize you, sir, as my prisoner.

It is the kiss of Judas, an expression of love with a parallel to hanging in it, like Polly's, that gives zest. Wine is normally used as a symbol of spiritual intoxication, but in this play the spirit is a sinister one, rather as the word *pleasure*, which it uses continually, always refers to the pleasures ("mystical" because connected with death-wishes) of cheating, or cruelty, or death. The five other uses, counting *pleased*, that I don't quote, are all of this sort. The doubtful one is Lockit's—

> Bring us then more liquor. To-day shall be for pleasure, to-morrow for business.

He has told the audience that he will make Peachum drunk and so have the pleasure of cheating him.

The more sinister because by making the pleasure of betrayal a mere condiment she claims that to her the affair is trivial—"What you can be made to feel heartbreaking I have the strength to judge rightly." Anyway the *zest* keeps us from thinking her so stupid as to be mercenary about it, which would be to feel nothing.

Peachum treats Macheath here with a sinister respect not chiefly intended as mockery; all politeness has an element of irony, but this is a recognition of the captain's claims; he is now half divine because fated to sacrifice.

> *P.* You must now, sir, take your leave of the ladies; and, if they have a mind to make you a visit, they will be sure to find you at home [and sure of the

"last pleasure" of seeing the execution. The preliminaries of death are a
failure in the sex war, since the ladies can no longer be deceived, even if
death itself is a triumph in it]. The gentleman, ladies, lodges in Newgate.
Constables, wait upon the captain to his lodgings.

> *Mac.* At the tree I shall suffer with pleasure,
>   At the tree I shall suffer with pleasure;
>   Let me go where I will
>   In all kinds of ill
>   I shall find no such furies as these are.

He can't go where he will—he expects to leave prison only for Hell. The
half-poetical, half-slang word *tree* applies both to the gibbet and to the
cross, where the supreme sacrificial hero suffered, with ecstasy.

> *Peachum.* Ladies, I'll take care the reckoning shall be discharged.
>   (Exit Macheath, guarded, with Peachum and constables.)

He, not they, is the fury, the avenging snake-goddess; to look after the
reckoning is his whole function towards both parties. The delicacy of his
irony (this, I think, is a rule about good ironies) is that it can safely
leave you guessing about both parties' consciousness of it; the more sincerely he treats Macheath as an aristocrat the more cruelly he isolates
him—

> *(In the condemned Hold.)*
> *Lockit.* Do but examine them, sir—never was better work—how genteelly
>   they are made. They will fit as easily as a glove, and the nicest gentleman
>   in England *might* not be ashamed to wear them. (He puts on the chains.)
>   If I had the best gentleman in the land in my custody, I could not equip
>   him more handsomely. And so, sir, I now leave you to your private medita-
>   tions.

—the less sincerely, the more he mocks—but at the whole notion of aristocracy that Macheath has aped into disaster. Thus even if the insincerity
was expressed grossly, so that Macheath could appeal through it to his
audience ("obviously you mean this, and it is unfair") he could still not
appeal against it as a personal insult ("I really *have* the virtues of the
aristocrat"); they would then be mocked, and he would have confessed
he was not one of them. Such an irony is a sort of intellectual imitation
of more valuable states of mind. To the opponent, there is no practical
use in distinguishing between whether the man is conscious or unconscious of his meaning—if he isn't he will be when he is told. "Oh, so you
thought that funny, did you? Well, I wasn't thinking of that special case,
but it seems to apply to that all right." The force of irony is its claim to
innocence; the reason for its wide usefulness is that the claim may still be
plausible when the man's consciousness of his irony is frank—"This is
the normal thing to feel; I felt this before I had met people like
you." . . .

I must go back to the betrayal scene.

Macheath. Was this well done, Jenny? Women are decoy ducks, who can
trust them? Beasts, jades, jilts, harpies, furies, whores.

He may mean that these women are whores, which is no discovery, or
that all women are, which is made plausible only by being half-said. The
climax, the worst he can say of them, is the obvious, which brings back a
sort of comedy to the strain of the scene. But its trenchant flatness also
makes us feel that the second meaning is obvious, though it would contradict the first (he could not blame them for being like everybody). Even
this is a sort of double irony.

"Was this well done?" belongs to Cleopatra in all the versions of her
story. It does not matter whether we take Macheath as quoting it (he
quotes Shakespeare a moment before) or re-inventing it, but it would be
wrong to take it only as a comic misuse of heroic dignity like Ancient
Pistol's; however queer the logic may be there should be a grand echo in
one's mind from the reply of Charmian:

> It is well done, and fitting for a princess
> Descended from so many mighty kings.

—indeed Peachum drives the point home at once:

> Your case, Mr. Macheath, is not particular; the greatest heroes have been
> undone by women.

The pleasure in seeing that two systems so different to emotion or morality as Antony and Macheath work in the same way is connected with the
Royal Society, but there are queerer forces in it than that.

Grand only by simplicity and concentration, and only by this grandeur
not normal colloquial English (so that it is a reliable phrase for Macheath), the question owes its tenseness to its peculiar assumptions; if it
is fitting the other person must have thought the act good, not merely
allowable, and yet must be capable of being made to see that it is wrong
by a mere appeal. So there must be a powerful and obvious clash of two
modes of judgment. When it is used to Cleopatra one must remember
that by choosing this death she destroys her children only to avoid a hurt
to her pride (not till her being carted in the triumph becomes certain
does the world become empty for her without Antony); that the soldier
who speaks feels that she has broken her word to Caesar; that Shakespeare's play has made us suspect her of planning to betray Antony, and
that some of her tantrums—dragging the messenger about by the hair—
can only have seemed comic, vulgar and wicked. Only by a magnificent
forcing of the sympathies of the audience is she made a tragic figure in
the last act. The sentence, then, used to her, means "You have cheated
Caesar and destroyed yourself; you think this heroic but it is childish; it is
like the way you cheated Antony till you destroyed him." It is because of

this suggestion that the answer of Charmian seems to call back and justify Cleopatra's whole life; all her acts were indeed like this one; all therefore fitting for a princess. It is a measure of the queerness of this alarming tragedy (no one can say how much irony there is in the barge speech) that the effect of the question is very little altered when it is "parodied" for the comic opera; both uses give a quasi-mystical "justification by death" which does not pretend to justify by normal standards.

So to explain the effect of the phrase here (it is a great effect) one has to invent queer but plausible reasons for thinking "This was well done." The most obvious is that the betrayal is poetic justice on him for being unfaithful to Polly; the structure of the play indeed insists on this. The first act gives the personal situation; we meet Polly, her parents at their business, finally Macheath, secretly married to her and hiding in the house. From his richly-prepared entry to the end of the first act he goes on swearing eternal faithfulness to her—"if you doubt it, let me stay—and be hanged." Two grand scenes of the second act then introduce us to the tribe of which these two are symbolic heroes, the society of which they are flowers (for Polly, unlike her parents, is "aristocratic" as well as "bourgeois")—to the eight thieves of Macheath's gang, which he dare not join since Polly's father is now his enemy, then to the eight whores he collects because he must be idle.

> I must have women—there is nothing unbends the mind like them; money is not so strong a cordial for the time.

Cordial, medicine for the heart, implies drink, which gives courage—love is an intoxication. To unbend your mind is to loosen the strong bow of your thought so that it will be strong in the next demand on it; a statesman's excuse for pleasure (indeed *the time* seems to imply "this unfortunate but no doubt brief period of history"); used here with a ludicrous or pathetic dignity whose very untruth has the gay dignity of intentional satire. Macheath, like Antony, like the ambitious politician, must unbend his mind because he must forget his fears. Into his statement of this fact, whose confession of fear frees it from bravado, he throws a further comparison to the avarice inherent in the life of safety he despises (so that these few words include both bourgeois and aristocrat); "to those who live within the law the mere possession of money is a sufficient intoxication." But however well he talks he is treating Polly with contempt:

> What a fool is a fond wench! Polly is most confoundedly bit. I love the sex; and a man who loves money might as well be contented with one guinea, as I with one woman.

(Satire on money justifies anything.)

> Do all we can, women will believe us; for they look upon a promise as an excuse for following their own inclinations.

("However frankly theatrical we make our professions of heroic love, professions which necessarily have the irony inherent in all fixed rules of politeness, such as are essential to civilisation.") It was the innocence and pathos of Polly in "oh ponder well," we are told, that swung round the audience on the first night. From the standpoint of heroic love the act was well done.

In any case the woman who really undoes him is not Jenny but Polly, however much against her will; unselfish love leads to honest marriage, and therefore Polly's father is determined to have him killed. It is love at its best that is the most fatal. This forces her to be like Cleopatra, and may make it poetic justice that he should betray her; anyway it removes much of the guilt from Jenny. And there is always, since this brings the thing nearer to a stock tragedy, the idea that it is in a fundamental way "well done" to cause the hero's death because it is necessary to the play.

But there is a more curious pathos in the question if one forgets about Polly, as Macheath has done. It is the questioner here who has both answers to the question in his mind. The "compliments" of the ladies to one another, through which he has sat placidly drinking, treat just such betrayals by Jenny only as acts of heroic self-control.

Mrs. Coaxer. If any woman hath more art than another, to be sure 'tis Jenny Diver. Though her fellow be never so agreeable, she can pick his pocket as coolly as if money were her only pleasure. Now that is a command of the passions uncommon in a woman.

Jenny. I never go to a tavern with a man but in the way of business. I have other hours, and other sort of men, for my pleasure. But had I your address, madam—

(On the face of things a prostitute is unlike other women in only wanting money. In this satire a prostitute is an independent woman who wants all the nobility included in the idea of freedom, and a chaste genteel woman only wants a rich marriage. If you hate Jenny for betraying the hero then she is actually as bad as a good woman, but Mrs. Coaxer assumes that she obviously can't be, and therefore that her behaviour on the crucial issue of money shows nobility; she is faithful to her sorority when she acts like this. Jenny's reply shows the humility of a truly heroic soul.)

Macheath. Have done with your compliments, ladies, and drink about. You are not so fond of me, Jenny, as you used to be.

Jenny. 'Tis not convenient, sir, to show my fondness before so many rivals. 'Tis your own choice, and not my inclination, that will determine you.

He cannot say she has deceived him. "What," he says as she enters:

And my pretty Jenny Diver too! as prim and demure as ever! There is not any prude, however high bred, hath a more sanctified look, with a more mischievous heart: ah, thou art a dear artful hypocrite!

He loves her for having the power to act as she so soon acts to him (there is a bitter gentility in it which he too feels to be heroic) both as a walking satire on the claims to delicacy of the fine ladies and as justified in her way of life by her likeness to the fine ladies, whose superiority he half admits.

> *Macheath.* . . . If any of the ladies choose gin, I hope they will be so free as to call for it.
> *Jenny.* You look as if you meant me. Wine is strong enough for me. Indeed, sir, I never drink strong waters but when I have the colic.
> *Macheath.* Just the excuse of the fine ladies! why, a lady of quality is never without the colic.

The colic as a justification for drinking is a disease like the spleen, half-mental, caused by a life of extreme refinement, especially as expressed by tight-lacing. It is because he so fully understands and appreciates her half-absurd charm that he is so deeply shocked by what should have been obvious, that it is a weapon frankly used against himself.

His respect for her is very near the general respect for independence; the main conflict in his question is that between individualism and the need for loyalty. In being a "beast of prey," the play repeats, she is like all humanity except in her self-knowledge and candour, which make her better. She is the test and therefore somehow the sacrifice of her philosophy; quasi-heroic because she takes a theory to its extreme; if wrong then because she was "loyal" to it. Macheath's question becomes "It is a fine thing when individuals like us can sustain themselves against society. But for that very reason we ought to hold together; surely it is not well done of you to prey upon *me*"—with the idea "I thought I could make her love me so much that I could disarm her." Jenny's answer is supplied by Mrs. Slammekin in her complaint at not sharing in the profits; "I think Mr. Peachum, after so long an acquaintance, might have trusted me as well as Jenny Diver"; she owes as much faith to the professional betrayer as to Macheath in his capacity of genteel rake, "martyr to the fair."

But Macheath does not believe in individualism in this sense; honour among thieves is taken for granted and only a boast by contrast with politicians. He believes his second arrest to be due to Jemmy Twitcher, and this seems really to shock him. The question does not simply mean (what is inherent in it) "we believe in all against all, but now I am horrified by it." It is only in matters of love that he has so nearly believed in all against all as to put a real shock into the question. He has really a sort of love for her (partly because she is against all). He has of course treated her with more contempt than Polly. So that the more serious you make their feelings for each other the more strongly you invoke the other notion, which applies also to Polly; not Independence but Love-Betrayal-

Death; "it is especially in all lovers that we see that all human beings, being independent, are forced to prey upon one another."

These notions must now be pursued into the character of Polly, where their irony is more subtle. She has been idealised ever since her first night. In the self-righteous sequel named after her, when they are all transported, Gay made Macheath a weak fish permanently in the clutches of Jenny Diver and Polly the only civilised character able to sustain the high tone demanded by the Noble Savage. Her first words in the play, at an entry for which our curiosity has been worked up for two and a half pages, make a rather different impression. She uses the same Comic Primness as her father and his clients—a friend of Richardson's told him he was too fond of "tarantalising" like Polly—and this delicate device in a dramatist may wish one to feel any shade of sympathy towards the speaker. You may say that this is a bold and subtle trick to defeat the tone of the play and bring on a real good heroine (if she is not careful she will seem a prig), or that she is defending her lover by a process unusual to her; so that the audience will have a pleasant surprise on discovering her true character. There is more in it than that.

> *Polly.* I know as well as any of the fine ladies how to make the most of myself and of my man too. A woman knows how to be mercenary, though she hath never been in a court or at an assembly. We have it in our natures, papa. If I allow Captain Macheath some trifling liberties, I have this watch and other visible marks of his favour to show for it. A girl who cannot grant some things, and refuse what is most material, will make a poor hand of her beauty, and soon be thrown upon the common.

(The common is the heath that her husband rules.)

This might be an attack on her under both heads, as making a false fine-lady claim and having real shopkeeper vices. She has two songs, and there are near two pages, containing the discovery that she is married, before she can safely be let speak again.

Peachum's remarks about her do not make up our minds for us—

> If the girl had the discretion of a court lady, who can have a dozen young fellows at her ear without complying with one, I should not matter it.

It is her innocence, which he admits, that is untrustworthy; it is a form of sensuality; especially because certain to change.

She does not say what is "most material," either from the modesty of virtue, the slyness of evil, or the necessity of deceiving her father; her real object may be to reform Macheath and make him an honest shopkeeper. One may take either way her classing the unmentioned marriage lines with the flaunted watch, and the dignity of its appearance among general terms may be pathetic from avarice or from a simple pride. "*We* have it in our natures, papa," either because theft is in our blood, or because our nature is to be intelligent as well as good, and could not reliably be good otherwise. This is an early example of the joke from Comic Primness about the innocent young girl, which runs on through Sheridan, Thackeray, Dodgson, and Wilde—that it is only proper for her to be worldly, because she, like the world, should know the value of her condition, and that there must be no question of whether she is conscious or not of being worldly, so that she is safe (much too safe) from your calling the bluff of her irony, because she deserves either not to be told of the cold judgments of the world or not to be reminded of them. "Make the most of my man" may mean "make the most money possible out of the man I am working on now" or "have the best influence I can on this man to whom my life is now bound"; nor would it be graceful in her to claim that the second is wholly unselfish and so distinguish it from the first. If she is able to deceive her father by this phrase it is a perquisite rightly due to the language of delicacy and understanding. Yet on the highest view of her she is absurd; what could any woman "make" of Macheath, already a limited perfection? To make him honest would be to make him mercenary. She might indeed (I suspect Gay ran away from this very ironical theme in *Polly*) make him a Virginian squire after transportation, as Moll Flanders did her "very fine gentleman, as he really is." The exquisite sense of freedom in one of the ballad lines used by the songs—"over the hills and far away"—is twisted into a romantic view of transportation by a remark of Polly just before. But she doesn't see her way to that now; she is not so placed as to have one purpose and one meaning.

Indeed the fascination of the character is that one has no means of telling whether she is simple or ironical; not merely because if ironical she would speak as if simple, but because if simple it would be no shock to her, it would be a mere shift of the conscious focus, to be told her meanings if ironical. The effect is that "the contradictions do not arise for her; she is less impeded than we are." This sort of thing usually requires complacence, and the Victorians did it very well, as in the mellowness of the jumps from spirituality to intrigue in Trollope's clerical death-scenes. Polly accepts her parents' wise advice, though she cannot live up to it, as readily as their high moral tone, as readily as she makes herself useful by telling lies to their customers; that she is so businesslike makes us believe in the vigour of her goodness; "real goodness knows that if its practice in an imperfect world is to be for the best its acts must be imperfect." She grants fully that her love is a weakness; her excuse for marriage even in a song has a delicate reserve in its double use of the inevitable criteria:

> I thought it both safest and best

is as near as a lyric will carry her to a moral claim. You may always think her as bad as they are. Her most shocking effects of pathos, like the play's best jokes, come from a firm acceptance of her parents' standards, which gives her the excuse always needed by poetry for a flat statement of the obvious. Circumstances make the low seem to her the normal, so she can use without affectation the inverted hypocrisy of Swift.

> *Peachum.* And had you not the common views of a gentlewoman in your marriage, Polly?
> *Polly.* I don't know what you mean, sir.
> *Peachum.* Of a jointure, and of being a widow. . . . Since the thing sooner or later must happen, I daresay the captain himself would like that we should get the reward for his death sooner than a stranger. . . .
> *Mrs. Peachum.* But your duty to your parents, hussy, obliges you to hang him. What would many a wife give for such an opportunity!
> *Polly.* What is a jointure, what is widowhood, to me? I know my heart, I cannot survive him.

No less rich background of irony would let us feel that this was true, and a discovery, and a confession, and yet not be too burlesque for us to feel seriously about her.

> *Mrs. P.* What! is the wench in love in earnest then? I hate thee for being particular. Why, wench, thou art a shame to thy sex.
> *Polly.* But, hear me, mother—if you ever loved—
> *Mrs. P.* These cursed playbooks she reads have been her ruin. One word more, hussy, and I shall knock your brains out, if you have any.

This playbook itself, as the moralists insisted, is as likely as the others, like them through its very idealism, to bring ruin. Mrs. Peachum does well to be angry and is right in her suspicion ("I find in the romance you lent me, that none of the great heroes was ever false in love"). But the objection to love is not merely that of Puritan virtue or bourgeois caution; independence is involved. Because love puts this supreme virtue in danger good faith is there most of all necessary, but because of "love-betrayal-death" is there least obtained. A still more searching point is made in dealing with the weaker and more violent Lucy.

> *Lockit.* And so you have let him escape, hussy—have you?
> *Lucy.* When a woman loves, a kind word, a tender look, can persuade her to anything, and I could ask no other bribe. [Love is a form of money, as contemptible and as easy to cheat with as another.]
> *Lockit.* Thou wilt always be a vulgar slut, Lucy. If you would not be looked upon as a fool, you should never do anything but upon the foot of interest. Those that act otherwise are their own bubbles.
> *Lucy.* But love, sir, is a misfortune that may happen to the most discreet woman, and in love we are all fools alike. Notwithstanding all that he swore, I am now fully convinced that Polly Peachum is actually his wife. Did I let him escape, fool that I was! to go to her? Polly will wheedle herself into his money; and then Peachum will hang him, and cheat us both.

One might think Independence a brutish ideal imposed by a false intellectualism. Lockit makes it a polite social trick, a decent hiding of the reality, to pretend that one is a beast of prey. It is from a social criterion that Lucy is told to be anti-social and not "vulgar." You may call this an admission that the ideal, as a defence of selfishness, does not meet the facts of human nature; the joke is that as a cynicism the thing refutes itself; but there is a joke too against Lockit and the conventions. We are left with an acceptance of Egoist ethical theory. And the philosophical joke fits naturally onto the social one; only the rogue or the aristocrat, only the independent character, can afford to see the truth about the matter.

We return here to the Senecan remark of Peachum: "Of all beasts of prey, mankind is the only sociable one." The reason for the breadth of this remark, its wide use for a cult of independence, is that it gives two contradictory adjectives to man. One cannot reduce it to a gangster blow-the-gaff sentiment, implying "see how tough I am." In the first place it may involve an appeal to individualist theory—"all actions apparently altruistic must have a solid basis in the impulses of the individual, and only so can be understood. They can only be based on self-love, because the individual is alone; there is merely nothing else for them to be based on. Only by facing this, by understanding the needs of the individual, can society be made safe." Secondly there is a more touching and less analytic idea—"all life is too painful for the impulses of altruism to be possible. To refuse to accept this is to judge your fellow creatures unjustly." That man should be made unique in this way is indeed a boast about his reason and the power that it gives to be independent; all the ramifications of irony that drive home and generalise this idea relate it to the central cult of the man who can stand alone. Of course the claim to be such a man is as pathetic in an Augustan thief as a Chicago tough, but the play makes us feel that.

For there is no doubt about the sociability. One of the most terrible of these comic scenes is that between Lucy and Polly, one attempting murder, the other suspecting it, and yet each finding "comfort" in each other's company. The play has made the word ready for them to wring the last ironies from it.

> *Peachum.* But make haste to Newgate, boy, and let my friends know what I intend; for I love to make them easy, one way or the other.
>
> *Filch.* When a gentleman is long kept in suspense, penitence may break his spirit ever after. Besides, certainty gives a man a good air upon his trial, and makes him risk another without fear or scruple. But I'll away, for 'tis a pleasure to be a messenger of comfort to friends in affliction.

Death is the comfort, for most, and it is a pleasure to tell them of it. Polly tells her mother she has married for love; she faints, thinking the girl had been better bred:

> *Peachum.* See, wench, to what a condition you have reduced your poor
> mother! A glass of cordial this instant! How the poor woman takes it to
> heart!
> (*Polly goes out, and returns with it.*)
> Ah hussy, now this is the only comfort your mother has left.
> *Polly.* Give her another glass, sir; my mother drinks double the quantity
> whenever she is out of order.

When she isn't, it is still her chief comfort. All this leads up to Lucy's
great scene.

> *Lucy.* . . . I have the ratsbane ready—I run no risk; for I can lay her death
> upon the gin, and so many die of that naturally, that I shall never be called
> in question. But say I were to be hanged—I never could be hanged for
> anything that would give me greater comfort than the poisoning that slut.

Death is certain anyhow, and its name is hanging throughout the play.

> (*Enter Polly.*)
> . . . Dear madam, your servant. I hope you will pardon my passion when
> I was so happy to see you last—I was so overrun with the spleen, that
> I was perfectly out of myself; and really when one hath the spleen, every-
> thing is to be excused by a friend.

The spleen is aristocratic, so her use of poison is also to be excused.
Their faults are always the result of their greatness of soul.

> *Lucy.* When a wife's in her pout
> (As she's sometimes, no doubt)
>   The good husband, as meek as a lamb,
>   Her vapours to still,
>   First grants her her will,
>   And the quieting draught is a dram;
> Poor man! and the quieting draught is a dram.
> I wish all our quarrels might have so comfortable a reconciliation.
> *Polly.* I have no excuse for my own behaviour, madam, but my misfortunes
> —and really, madam, I suffer too upon your account.

Polly's polite claim to altruism, whether or not it has a sincerity which
would only be pathetic, acts as an insult, and the dram ("in the way of
friendship") is immediately proposed. Lucy is leading up to the poison
in the song, but her diplomacy is so stylised as to become a comment of
the author's. The quieting draught is death; no other medicine will bring
peace or comfort to so restless a fragment of divinity. It is also alcohol;
peace can only be obtained from what gives further excitement, because
simple peace is not attainable in the world. Gin alone, however, she has
just pointed out, is often enough quieting in the fullest sense, and the
poetic connection between death and intoxication gives a vague rich memory of the blood of the sacrament and the apocalyptic wine of the wrath
of God.

Poor man. He is a martyr to the fair, so that his weaknesses are due to his modish greatness of spirit; when a man takes this tone about himself he means that he considers himself very successful with women, and pays them out. Lucy is boasting of the strength of the spleen as a weapon against him. Poor man, more generally, because of the fundamental human contradictions that are displayed; he is a beast of prey forced to be sociable. And "poor man, in the end he kills her, and is no doubt hanged"—for the force of *and,* prominent and repeated, is to make giving a quieting draught something quite different from, and later than, the attempt to "give her will"—it might be only drink she willed for, and the attempt to give it once for all was anyway hopeless. The comparison of the dramatic and condemned thing—murder by poison—to the dull and almost universal one—quieting by drink—is used to show that the dramatic incident is a symbol or analysis of something universal. Afterwards (the double irony trick) this both refutes itself and insists on its point more suggestively (appears analysis not symbol) by making us feel that the dramatic thing is itself universal—the good meek husband, whether by poison or plain gin, is as much a murderer as Lucy. From whatever cause there is a queer note of triumph in the line.

The attempted murder is called a "comfort" chiefly because it is no more; to kill Polly won't get her back Macheath. And it fails because she finds Polly is not happy enough to deserve it; at the crucial moment Macheath is brought back in chains. There is no more need for murder in Lucy, because Macheath seems to have despised Polly's help, and anyway is separated from her. There is no more hope of "comfort" for Polly; she tosses gin and death together to the floor. So both women are left to poison his last moments. The playwright then refuses to kill Macheath, from the same cheerful piercing contempt; he is not dignified enough, he tells the audience, "though you think he is," to be made a tragic hero. Lucy's attempt is useless except for its ill-nature, which makes it seem a "typically human" and therefore pathetic piece of folly; she takes up an enthusiasm for murder because otherwise she would have to admit the facts (which the human creature can never afford to do) and give way to the "spleen" and despair—the spleen which is the despair of the most innocent and highly refined characters because to such characters this existence is essentially inadequate. Lucy's comic vanity in taking this tone (as in Macheath's different use of the device) is displayed only to be justified; "what better right has anyone else to it?"; it is not denied, such is the pathos of the effect, that the refined ladies may well take this tone, but they must not think it a specially exalted one. (To the Freudian, indeed, it is the human infant to whose desires this life is essentially inadequate; King Lear found a mystical pathos in the fact that the human infant, alone among the young of the creatures, is subject to impotent fits of fury.) It is this clash and identification of the refined, the universal, and the low that is the whole point of pastoral.

For the final meaning of this play, whose glory it is to give itself so wholeheartedly to vulgarisation, I can only list a few approaches to its irony. "I feel quite grateful to these fools; they make me feel sure I am right because they are so obviously wrong" (in this hopeful form satire is widely used to "keep people going" after loss of faith); "having got so far towards sympathy with the undermen, *non ragioniam di lor*, lest we come down to the *ultima ratio*" (Voltaire not talking politics to his valet); "one can see how impossible both the thieves and the politicians are if one compares them to heroes" (the polite literary assumption; the pose of detachment); "low as these men are, the old heroes were like them, and one may well feel the stronger for them; life was never dignified, and is still spirited." (The good spirits of Fielding making a Homeric parody of a village scuffle.) "The old heroes were much more like the modern thief than the modern aristocrat; the present order of society is based on an inversion of real values" (Pope sometimes made rather fussy local satire out of this); "this is always likely to happen; everything spiritual and valuable has a gross and revolting parody, very similar to it, with the same name; only unremitting effort can distinguish between them" (Swift); "this always happens; no human distinction between high and low can be accepted for a moment; Christ on earth found no fit company but the thieves" (none of them accepted the full weight of the anarchy of this, but none of them forgot it; perhaps the mere easiness of Gay makes one feel it in him most easily). It is a fine thing that the play is still popular, however stupidly it is enjoyed.

From *The Augustans*

by Maynard Mack

. . . A further element of parody in the *Opera* is literary. It will be noticed that the Lucy-Polly episodes are a mock rendering of the stock dramatic revenge theme, and that the affair of Macheath and Polly offers a burlesque version of the standard stage conflict of love and duty. Moreover, the plot laughingly suggests in its main outlines the pattern of Aristotelian tragedy, which calls for a great man's fall through a tragic weakness. To this end, Macheath is set somewhat apart from the other characters as a "great man" (this was also contemporary slang for Wal-

"From The Augustans," *by Maynard Mack. This selection is from "Gay: The Beggar's Opera," in the "Introduction" by Maynard Mack to* The Augustans, *2nd ed., English Masterpieces Series, Vol. 5 (Englewood Cliffs, N.J.: Prentice-Hall, Inc., 1961), pp. 17–19. First published in 1950. Reprinted by permission of the author and Prentice-Hall, Inc.*

pole); tag ends from Shakespeare are put in his mouth; and he is supplied
with a tragi-comic flaw in the form of a weakness for women. As the play
progresses, however, we begin to realize that this parody of tragic pattern
is not simply a lighthearted joke, but the focus of the play's most serious
implications. For Macheath's weakness for women proves to be a way of
dramatizing a more paradoxical flaw in this "hero": the error of supposing that the society he moves in honors any values except money. The
satire of Macheath, in short, turns into satire of a world where everything
is for sale.

Gay builds up this world in a brilliant variety of ways. We are introduced at the very beginning to Peachum going over his account book
—the basic symbol of a price-society. As he and his wife and his servant
Filch speak, we notice the persistence of the language of business: "property," "profit," "employment," "customer," "interest," "credit," "bank-
notes." We notice too the prevalence of what Gay's age called cant: a
hollow jargon of piety, associated mainly (as also by Falstaff in I Henry
IV) with the Puritans, who composed in large part the trading middle
classes. So Peachum loves to make his friends "easy" (I ii). Filch asserts
the pleasure of being "the messenger of comfort to friends in affliction"
(I ii). Mrs. Peachum acknowledges the "frailty of an over-scrupulous
conscience" (I iv) (in shrinking from murder). She dispatches Filch—
"since you have nothing better to do" (I iv)—to learn his catechism, and
urges him not to lie because she hates a liar. In the same way, she is re-
spectably upset by her daughter's "ruin" (I viii).

This middle-class price taint is not confined to the Peachums. Lockit
shows it equally, and both Peachum and Lockit constantly reach out in
their observations to identify their standards with those of the whole
society: "We and the surgeons are more beholden to women than all the
professions besides"; "What business hath he to keep company with lords
and gentlemen? he should leave them to prey upon one another"; "My
daughter to me should be, like a court lady to a minister of state, a key
to the whole gang" (I iv); "A lawyer is an honest employment; so is mine"
(I i). Even the highwaymen make their contribution to this picture: "Why
are the laws leveled at us? Are we more dishonest than the rest of mankind?" "The world is avaricious, and I hate avarice" (II i).

Dramatically, this standard of price serves the purpose of discrimi-
nating between the characters. Peachum and Lockit are wholly infected,
and accept their world quite frankly on its own terms. The thieves, ironically, are somewhat less tainted, mitigating the price standard with ideals
of courage, magnanimity, and (for a time) loyalty. They take pride in
the fact that they would not betray a friend, that they are freehearted
in the use of money, and that "what we win, gentlemen, is our own by
the law of arms and the right of conquest" (II i). The latter is Gay's application of a familiar imperialistic *cliché* to a context which reveals its
hollowness; but as compared with Peachum and Lockit, we can see that

the thieves have a slight moral edge: they are not miserly, they risk their lives for their winnings, and all but one of them proves to be loyal. Macheath is still less tainted than the other thieves. Competing with love of money in his case are an aristocratic consciousness of "honor"—"These are the tools of men of honor. Cards and dice are only fit for cowardly cheats" (II iv)—and a romantic interest in "love"—"I must have women. . . . Money is not so strong a cordial for the time" (II iii). We must not forget that Macheath is always a comic character, only a parody hero; but we must not overlook, either, the various associations with which Gay surrounds him: Mrs. Trapes's Pilate-like washing of hands (III vi); Jenny's Judas-kiss of betrayal (II iv); the fact that he, unlike anyone else in the play, reacts with moral anger at this evidence of the ways of the world; that he is associated, by Peachum, even though comically, with "the greatest heroes"; that he freely proffers his purse to his colleagues; and that he is really surprised when one of his own gang peaches him— an unwelcome "proof that the world is all alike."

The chief purpose of the price standard, however, is to provide the environment with which those who are not wholly infected by its struggle, and before which they all have to admit defeat. Thus Macheath is twice betrayed for his error in supposing that "love" (Jenny Diver) or loyalty (Jemmy Twitcher) might be above price. Polly likewise (a parody of romantic ideals as Macheath is of heroic ones) sins before the *mores* of her world in refusing to be a prostitute: she seems dangerous and dishonest to the Peachums because she proposes to be honest. Even the standard above money by which she and Lucy are motivated in their passion for Macheath proves, in this environment, to have a large infusion of self-interest. Their quarrel over him, and Lucy's design to poison Polly, simply enact at another level the cut-throat competition that everywhere prevails.

And in the end, this society requires even the beggar poet who (professedly) has composed the play to put his integrity on sale. He had intended, he tells us (III xvi), to exhibit Macheath and all the other personages of the drama either hanged or transported; but "the taste of the town" will not permit this. Blind to the catastrophe of a culture rotted through with "business" values, the audience is hypersensitive to the "catastrophe" in plays. And the artist (naturally in a society like this a *beggar-poet*), though he knows that moral values ought to prevail, has no recourse but to discard them and bring literature into line with life. This is the "down-right deep Tragedy," profoundly serious as well as comical, of *The Beggar's Opera*.

From *To the Palace of Wisdom*

by Martin Price

In *The Beggar's Opera* we find once again a symmetrical disposition of characters. The play opens with a fine presentation of the inverted mercantile world of the Peachums. This world operates by the cash nexus alone, but it assumes its values with prim respectability. The tone of the play is extraordinarily complex, as William Empson has shown: the Peachums present an outrageously straight-faced assertion of thorough acquisitiveness with all the false unction of bourgeois stuffiness. So straight-faced is their parody of the conduct of their betters that they create a world highly formalized and "rhetorical." Their speeches, like all those in the play, suggest that no man can endure to think as little of himself as he deserves; all must console themselves with some form of righteous cant. Their use of this cant is so handsomely stylized that it never quite seems the conventional self-deception men need in real life; instead, it has, as they perform, a delicious absurdity, with a constant undertone of bitter wit as one applies it to the actualities the play never directly admits.

This is, perhaps, a roundabout way of getting at a unique effect. The play invites us at once to enjoy freedom from moral judgment and accept the comic ease of this world, where the "paradox of trade and morality" is so easily resolved into the values of trade and the gestures of morality. In this aspect, it is like those comic and pastoral works (it was undertaken, at Swift's urging, as a "Newgate pastoral") in which the conflicts of moral existence are banished. Yet, at every point, the play creates a satiric simplification of the conduct that governs the "high" world of Walpole and the court. Neither of these aspects—the comic and the satiric—can be ignored. The pastoral simplicity is not virtue opposed to a corrupt and complex court, but corruption reduced to artless ease, its humbug so effortless and thoroughgoing that it seems to criticize only the ineptitude of actual hypocrites. One may recall Pope's emphasis on the healthy freedom that dares "laugh out"; there is a relief in the comparative decency of frank assertion, even when it is presented by characters who pretend not to recognize its import. Gay's method can, I think, be traced back to such a work as Swift's *Argument against Abolish-*

"*From* To the Palace of Wisdom," *by Martin Price. This selection is from "Orders and Forms," Chapter 8 of* To the Palace of Wisdom: Studies in Order and Energy from Dryden to Blake, *by Martin Price (Garden City, N.Y.: Doubleday & Company, Inc., 1964), pp. 245–49. A footnote has been omitted. Copyright © 1964 by Martin Price. Reprinted by permission of the author.*

ing Christianity, where the projector offers the comfortable meaning-lessness of "nominal Christianity" in opposition to a strenuous and un-reliable effort to legislate Christianity out of existence. It is a method, as I have suggested, that Mandeville used as well.

The Peachum household anticipates the family of Clarissa Harlowe in its righteous distrust of the aristocrat: he is not only dissolute, he is unpredictable, for he observes standards they cannot admit. Polly stands out as a creature who is spontaneous and unguarded. She has been se-duced by a mock aristocrat who has lent her romances (the counterpart of Millamant's reading in the Cavalier poets); they have opened visions of a more generous life than her parents can conceive. Polly's last words in the first act catch very well a self-dramatizing rhetoric, an unconscious identifying of herself with the romance heroine: "O how I fear! how I tremble!—Go—but when safety will give you leave, you will be sure to see me again; for 'till then Polly is wretched." This note of the romantic and histrionic is present earlier, as Polly considers Macheath's possible end:

> Methinks I see him already in the cart, sweeter and more lovely than the nosegay in his hand!—I hear the crowd extolling his resolution and intrepidity!—What vollies of sighs are sent from the windows of Holborn, that so comely a youth should be brought to disgrace! I see him at the tree! The whole Circle are in tears!—even Butchers weep! (I, xii.)

There is a telling difference between this ardent mixture of alarm and erotic daydream and the crisp finality of Mrs. Peachum's, "Hang your husband, and be dutiful," or Peachum's sententious, "The comfort-able estate of widowhood, is the only hope that keeps up a wife's spirits." Polly's emotion is more generous; it comes closer to the full range of human feeling than any other in the play, and it is reduced to a degree of comic unreality by its literary quality, its air of being something newly learned and not wholly mastered, however sincerely spoken. Gay makes romantic love a kind of child's masquerade in this world, as opposed to the more knowing game the elders seem to be playing.

But Polly herself suffers as the symmetry of the play develops. The second act gives us the world of the outlaw. The Gang are men who risk their lives for what they get. They depend upon each other for their safety, and their dependence builds a loyalty beyond the appeal of in-terest. They are at once more careless and more generous than the elder Peachums, and they live by a code of honor to which they trust their survival. It is in their swaggering boast of their purpose that their spirit of freedom is best stated:

> We retrench the superfluities of mankind. The world is avaritious, and I hate avarice. A covetous fellow, like a Jack-daw, steals what he was never made to enjoy, for the sake of hiding it. These are the robbers of mankind, for money was made for the full-hearted and generous, and where is the

injury of taking from another, what he hath not the heart to make use of? (II, i.)

The opposition of avarice and generosity sets up the central contrast of the play and prepares us for Macheath's disclosure: "Polly is most confoundedly bit.—I love the sex. And a man who loves money might as well be contented with one guinea, as I with one woman" (II, iii). Just as Polly is free of the grasping avarice of her parents, so Macheath is free of the possessive loyalty of her love. He is a natural aristocrat, a man of style: "I must have women. There is nothing unbends the mind like them." And his treatment of his doxies shows a fine sense of tone, a feeling for the manner of address each must have. Macheath is even more unguarded than Polly: he is incapable of any surrender of his freedom. He has no higher use for it than to enjoy it, certainly; but his love of the sex, like his captaincy of a gang of outlaws, makes his life the more precarious. If his love of women be the "flaw" in his mock-tragic character, the pursuit of freedom is perhaps its more serious basis, and, curiously, the quality that makes him more romantic than any of Polly's daydreams. Gay insists upon him as a somewhat shabby seducer and a tavern swell, but the "high" note Macheath somewhat fastidiously borrows from Shakespeare ("If musick be the food of Love, play on," from *Twelfth Night*; and paraphrasing *Antony and Cleopatra*: "Was this well done, Jenny?") alludes to a vanished nobility as surely as do the gestures of the playing cards in *The Rape of the Lock*.

Once the symmetry of Peachum and Lockit is established, Macheath's solitary career is set between paired characters as tenacious as manacles: the mercenary fathers and the possessive daughters. "If you had been kind to me 'till death," exclaims Polly, "it would not have vex'd me— And that's no very unreasonable request (though from a wife) to a man who hath not above seven or eight days to live" (II, xiii). The girls are simpler, far less assured and deft in their intrigues, but they are in some measure their fathers' daughters. Macheath, on the other hand, for all his operatic self-dramatization and self-pity, comes to a stark awareness that is all but tragic. "That Jemmy Twitcher should peach me, I own surpriz'd me!—'Tis a plain proof that the world is all alike, and that even our Gang can no more trust one another than other people. Therefore, I beg you, gentlemen, look well to yourselves, for in all probability you may live some months longer" (III, xiv). It is too much to say that he comes to accept his own nature as part of this world's, but the firm understatement would serve such a meaning in another kind of play.

Gay's lovers, then, seem to divide, Polly into the way of organized society, with its legal bonds and imprisoning institutions, Macheath into the way of outlawry, freedom from involvement, and therefore utter vulnerability. As Lockit puts it, "Of all animals of prey, man is the only sociable one. Every one of us preys upon his neighbours, and yet we herd together." But the play cannot end so, and the beggar imposes upon it an ending such as the taste of the town requires. The beggar's manipulation is, in one sense, a symbolic selling out in key with the world he has presented.

But even before this last insistence upon artifice is made, Gay has over-turned Macheath's moment of tragic eloquence with the introduction of four more wives, "with a child a-piece." Macheath dwindles from a noble solitary to a master of ineptitude, and the way is clear for a return to sentiment: "I take Polly for mine.—And for life, you Slut,—for we were really marry'd." We are back in the world of comedy, where the exceptional hero is as much fool as prophet, and where Polly's bungling goodness of heart finds its appropriate reward. The lovers are lovers, after all, and Macheath's seeming superiority to the captivity of marriage has been part of the somewhat tawdry swagger of a role too big to sustain. Polly, who has neither her parents' art nor Macheath's grandeur, has captured this world for bourgeois romance. What gives the play part at least of its peculiar force is Gay's willingness to explore conflicting views to the uttermost; they must be resolved by contrivance, finally, but the contrivance seems, after all, the inevitable. Macheath is not "lost above" this world; but he has been allowed to enjoy the histrionic illusion for a while. And Polly is not simply the helpless victim of a savage world; she has the tenacity of her parents without their coldness. These characters never begin to know themselves, nor do they control their fate; but Gay, like Fielding later, plays the just god in his creation.

From *Comedy and Society*
from Congreve to Fielding

by John Loftis

Because dramatists in the late seventeenth and earlier eighteenth centuries were indifferent to ideas with bold implications in political theory, it is easy to overestimate the originality of dramatists after 1728 in exploring social questions. Scarcely any English comedy in the thirty-five years before the appearance of *The Beggar's Opera* contained a hint that

"*From* Comedy and Society from Congreve to Fielding," *by John Loftis. This selection is from "The Displacement of the Restoration Tradition, 1728–1737," Chapter 5 of* Comedy and Society from Congreve to Fielding, *by John Loftis, Stanford Studies in Language and Literature, Vol. 19 (Stanford, Calif.: Stanford University Press, 1959), pp. 108–10. Reprinted by permission of the publisher.*

the hierarchical order of English society—with its immense and, to the twentieth-century mind, shocking inequalities of wealth, privilege, and opportunity—was not an inalienable condition of life. The tradition of genteel comedy deriving from the Restoration, with its focus on the narrow spectrum of society in which the gentry and the nobility mingled, perpetuated the social assumptions of the group that provided its subject, a conservative group that had nothing to gain by change. Not until the 1730's did dramatists generally acknowledge the merchants' claim to social consideration, and even then most of the dramatists gave no evidence of discarding their assumption of the rightness of a hierarchical social order: they merely acknowledged wealth and mercantile prominence as entitlements to high place.

In *The Beggar's Opera* there is a hint, perhaps on Gay's part an unintentional hint, of bolder views.[1] Gay's nominal subject is, of course, low life. The effectiveness of the play depends on the distance he establishes between the moral and social orders of the dramatic action and those of the lives of his contemporaries. The characters live with indifference to conventional moral and social discriminations, an indifference that could force the audience to consider what was usually taken for granted. Gay's beggars, observing irrationalities in English customs with an incredulous detachment, serve a literary function analogous to that of the eighteenth-century imaginary travelers: Montesquieu's Persian gentleman, Swift's Gulliver, Voltaire's Micromégas, and Goldsmith's Chinese gentleman, among others. The beggars, like the travelers, have the emotional detachment of outsiders and the resultant perspicacity; and they have, also like the travelers, the privilege of uninhibited comment granted to those who are totally uncommitted to the society that provides their subject.

We should be more inclined to see bold social comment in *The Beggar's Opera* had the subsequent history of England produced a revolution. Our view of history, conditioned by the analogy of organic evolution, leads us to evaluate earlier events—including such literary events as *The Beggar's Opera*—with reference to what happened later. England, unlike France, maintained its hierarchical, aristocratic structure throughout the eighteenth century. Consequently, we are led to emphasize eighteenth-century French social protests appearing in imaginative literature and to overlook parallel English instances. Certainly French literature of social criticism was more sustained, more eloquent, and more forthright than the English, just as it was more effective in producing action. Still, the continuing English conservatism leads us to underestimate the intensity of the protest against social inequalities by such writers as Gay, Fielding, and Dodsley.

Gay in *The Beggar's Opera* submits class relationships to scrutiny

---

1 Cf. Bertrand H. Bronson, *"The Beggar's Opera,"* in *Studies in the Comic* (University of California Publications in English, 1941), pp. 227–29.

through the device of inverting them: the lowest class, that of the high-waymen and beggars, is assumed to be of more consequence than the highest, that of the gentlemen and peers who govern the nation. This simple inversion, maintained without falter, carries the burden of Gay's social critique, which is not the less effective for its simplicity. No elaborate argument was needed to make the point that men, whatever their station, are fundamentally alike: that accidents of birth and fortune, more than differences in virtue and abilities, accounted for the immense discrepancies of privilege in the eighteenth century. The bare structure of *The Beggar's Opera* had subversive implications—and it was indeed deemed to be subversive by some eighteenth-century critics.[2]

It was the immense popularity of *The Beggar's Opera* that made it a strong dramatic and political force; and its popularity was a consequence of a fusion of topical and more generalized satire, all of it assimilated in a deftly turned musical play. Not a political allegory, *The Beggar's Opera* nevertheless conveys sustained criticism of Walpole, who is variously suggested in the characters of Macheath the highwayman, Peachum the "screen," and Robin of Bagshot, one of the lesser thieves. All of these characters move in a mock-heroic world (by implication the world of Walpole's government) in which peculation, bribery, and treachery are conditions of life. The fusion of topical denunciation with generalized social criticism gives intensity to the whole. Where, in other writers, the topical and the generalized are not joined, the former often seems trivial and the latter effete.

[2] Cf. an open letter printed in the *Daily Gazeteer*, May 7, 1737. In his life of Gay, Samuel Johnson discusses the contemporary charges that *The Beggar's Opera* had a pernicious influence.

From *English Theatre Music*
in the Eighteenth Century

by Roger Fiske

During the first quarter of the eighteenth century conventions similar to those of Italian operas in other countries were quickly established in

"From English Theatre Music in the Eighteenth Century," *by Roger Fiske. This selection is from "English Masque versus Italian Opera, 1695–1720" and "Ballad Opera, 1728–1736," Chapters 1 and 3 of* English Theatre Music in the Eighteenth Century, *by Roger Fiske (London: Oxford University Press, 1973), pp. 62–63, 66, 98–99. Copyright © Oxford University Press 1973. Extracted by permission of the author. Reprinted by permission of the author and the publisher.*

London. Opera plots, which at the start of the century had usually included one or two comic characters, became in general more serious and more unreal. Librettos, often adapted from earlier operas by other composers, purported to be about heroic figures in ancient legend or in ancient history, but often bore no relation to what we today know of the subject. Atalanta runs no race in Handel's opera of that name, and a reading of Xenophon is no help towards an understanding of *Serse*. Events always occur, or are described, during the often-very-long recitatives. Nothing ever happens during the arias and ensembles, which express at length a mood arising out of the situation left in mid-air at the end of the previous recitative. Plots had to be sufficiently complex to allow each of the main characters to sing arias in a wide variety of moods, and it was the expression of these moods rather than what happened that the audience enjoyed. The number of arias sung by each character was controlled by a sort of etiquette all too well understood by the castrati. As the Venetian playwright and librettist Goldoni put it,

> The three principal personages of the drama ought to sing five airs each; two in the first act, two in the second, and one in the third. The second actress and the second soprano can have only three, and the inferior characters must be satisfied with a single air each, or two at the most. The author of the words must furnish the musician with the different shades which form the *chiaroscuro* of music, and take care that two pathetic airs do not succeed one another. He must distribute with the same precaution the bravura airs, the airs of action, the inferior airs, and the minuets and rondeaus. He must, above all things, avoid giving impassioned airs, bravura airs, or rondeaus, to inferior characters.[1]

Hampered by such restrictions, it is not surprising that librettists seldom produced a dramatic situation that was both credible and lively.

With so few people able to understand Italian, the events would have had no impact on the audience but for the publication of librettos that included an English translation. . . . Operas always ended with a reconciliation scene, during which the villains were forgiven and undertook to reform their ways. Londoners were used to such endings in the plays of John Fletcher, but in operas they were more absurd because they were unmotivated.

The arias, especially those sung by the great castrati, were the main attraction. There was always a "chorus" of principals at the end, and perhaps one or two duets and ensembles, but arias predominated overwhelmingly over other musical forms. Handel towered over his contemporaries because his vocal lines and accompaniments constantly gave emotional depth to conventional lyrics and situations. Much more than his contemporaries, he thought dramatically, and even descriptively. Most of his arias were in *Da Capo* form, with the long opening section repeated

1 Goldoni's *Memoirs,* Eng. ed. 1814, i, pp. 185–6, quoted in 'The Aria in Opera Seria, 1725–1780,' by M. F. Robinson, *RMA Proceedings,* 1961–2.

after a middle section that was usually short and sometimes perfunctory. This repeat encouraged the singers to add difficult decorations and flourishes of their own devising, and audiences revelled in the skill with which they transformed the original vocal line into something rich and strange. . . .

There was never in England a widespread enthusiasm for Italian Opera. As in more recent years, it affected only a coterie of society people and intellectuals; the middle and lower class theatregoer inevitably preferred the playhouses where he could understand the words. But opera in a foreign tongue has always had a strong snob appeal for those few who wish to be thought cleverer than they are. Even if they could make nothing of the music, there was the fascination of watching those only-just-mentionable creatures, the castrati, strutting about in their monstrous pride. It is doubtful if Italian opera would ever have got established without them. Castrati had the additional allure of being foreign, and dozens of quotations can be produced to show that in the eighteenth and indeed the nineteenth centuries it was widely believed that foreigners by their very nature were better at music than Britons.

Yet the appeal of Italian Opera to intellectuals was fully justified. Handel's music was of superb quality, a quality that could seldom be matched in the playhouses, and castrato singing had a thrill about it that could never be matched in the playhouses. . . .

We have already seen that D'Urfey's *Wonders in the Sun* included a few popular song tunes, as also did one or two plays of the previous century. But the vast number in *The Beggar's Opera* must have seemed its most original feature. People associated opera with a succession of long arias whose music was hard to grasp and whose words were incomprehensible, and it was piquant, perhaps even funny, to have an opera whose tunes were short and familiar, and whose words made good sense. The plot too was as far removed as might be imagined from those used by Handel, Bononcini, and Ariosti. Instead of cardboard heroes of antiquity, Gay offered very real modern Londoners; instead of noble sentiments, every crime in the calendar. In fact he satirized Italian opera in the main by upending both its musical style and its moral flavour.

There are also some incidental digs. In the Introduction the Beggar remarks that he has provided the two ladies with parts of equal weight, and it was well known that Handel's great sopranos, Faustina and Cuzzoni, had recently insisted on just this. He also mentions with pride that he has "introduc'd the Similies that are in all your celebrated Operas; The Swallow, The Moth, The Ship, The Bee, The Flower," and these can in fact be found in Airs 34, 4, 10, 15, and 6 respectively. The Simile Aria was a great feature of Italian opera at this period, and the airs in which Polly compares herself to a ship and a swallow are not so much skits as copies of the real thing. . . .

Gay's final slap at Italian Opera comes at the end, when realism is suddenly abandoned, and the actors step outside their roles in order to contrive a wholly incredible happy ending. The effect is hard to bring off today, for few people know enough about what is being satirized. But in 1728 Macheath's absurd reprieve, totally unprepared for by anything said or done earlier, must have seemed a brilliant stroke to an audience familiar with the endings of Handel and Bononcini operas, in which men consistently evil for two acts and three-quarters suddenly reformed their whole mode of life and found love for a more convenient woman so that everyone should live happily ever after. As the Beggar puts it, "In this kind of drama, 'tis no matter how absurdly things are brought about," and the Player soon realizes that "All this we must do, to comply with the taste of the town."

The Shepherd as Gamester: Musical Mock-Pastoral in *The Beggar's Opera*

by Eric Kurtz

To take the customary view of *The Beggar's Opera* as the decisive battle in the war against Italian opera obscures a vital connection between Gay's ballad opera and the late-seventeenth-century theatrical masque, which found its finest expression in the musical drama of Henry Purcell. *The Beggar's Opera* is not so much an attack on Italian absurdities as it is an independent reassertion of a native tradition of musical drama which characteristically exposes its own artifices and tests them by incorporating mock-pastoral formulas into the larger pastoral genre.

The genre of pastoral is inherently playful, a literary game in which one pretends, in a sophisticated way, to be simple, in order artfully to celebrate artlessness. Since an awareness of the game is a large part of the fun, pastoral works often call attention to their own conventions, and test them by exposing their artifice. One characteristic device is to jostle one version of pastoral against another, as in Shakespeare's *As You Like It,* for example, where the various groups of characters—the Arcadian shepherds, the country bumpkins, the toughly sentimental young lovers —serve as touchstones for one another's authenticity, or lack of it. Another is to apply the conventions of pastoral to the wrong kind of low

―――――

"The Shepherd as Gamester: Musical Mock-Pastoral in The Beggar's Opera," *by Eric Kurtz.* © *1975 by Eric Kurtz. Used by permission of the author. This article appears in print for the first time in this volume. It was adapted by the author from a paper delivered before the New England College English Association on April 26, 1969.*

life, as in Gay's *Shepherd's Week* and *Trivia,* and his "Newgate pastoral,"
The Beggar's Opera.

These mock-pastoral devices can be found in numerous literary versions of pastoral, but they are particularly prominent in the antimasques
which occupied an increasingly large part of the courtly masques of the
early seventeenth century and which continued to be popular in the
theaters after the Restoration. Shirley's *The Triumph of Peace* (1634) is
a good instance, since its antimasque, consisting of almost twenty dances,
contains material that anticipates the pastoral and mock-pastoral elements in Purcell's operas and in *The Beggar's Opera.* The antimasque
opens in a tavern with a dance for the master of the tavern, a "maque-
relle"—that is, a pimp—two wenches, and two "wanton gamesters." This
is followed by a dance for various birds, and then a scene in which a
merchant is robbed and the thieves are taken by a constable and officers.
A dance for nymphs and satyrs follows, interrupted by four huntsmen,
and the antimasque ends with Don Quixote making attempts upon a
windmill. Even without the music or the elaborate details of the dances,
the surviving summary of the action makes clear the playful paradoxes
of this self-conscious genre.

Perhaps the best way to show what became of this tradition of musical
pastoral in the operas of Purcell and Gay is to trace a specific borrowing,
Purcell's popular song "If love's a sweet passion," and to look at its context in *The Beggar's Opera* and in its original setting, Purcell's *Fairy
Queen* (1692).

As Act III of *The Beggar's Opera* opens, Lockit scolds his daughter
Lucy for helping Macheath to escape from prison, but consoles himself
with the thought that Lucy may have coaxed Macheath into a better
"bargain" than he himself might have extorted. Lucy knows that love is
a calculated economic transaction, and usually a dishonest one, but she
insists on the real value of her love: "You know, Sir," she says, "I am
fond of him, and would have given money to have kept him with me."
Then follows this dialogue and Lucy's song, which insists equally on a
cynical and a sentimental view of love:

> *Lock.* Ah, *Lucy*! thy education might have put thee more upon thy guard;
> for a girl in the bar of an Alehouse is always besieg'd.
> *Lucy.* Dear Sir, mention not my education—for 'twas to that I owe my ruin.

> ### Air XLI. *If Love's a sweet passion, &c.*
> When young at the bar you first taught me to score,
> And bid me be free with my lips, and no more;
> I was kiss'd by the Parson, the Squire, and the Sot:
> When the guest was departed, the kiss was forgot.
> But his kiss was so sweet, and so closely he prest,
> That I languish'd and pin'd 'till I granted the rest.

> If you can forgive me, Sir, I will make a fair confession, for to be sure
> he hath been a most barbarous villain to me.

Lock. And so you have let him escape, hussy—have you?

Lucy. When a woman loves; a kind look, a tender word can persuade her to any thing—and I could ask no other bribe.

Lock. Thou wilt always be a vulgar slut, *Lucy*—If you would not be look'd upon as a fool, you should never do any thing but upon the foot of interest. Those that act otherwise are their own bubbles.

Lucy. But Love, Sir, is a misfortune that may happen to the most discreet woman, and in love we are all fools alike.

The financial metaphors have given complicated meanings to that last conventional statement, "Love, Sir, is a *misfortune* that may happen to the most *discreet* woman." The song and the situation have both mocked any simple view of her innocent feelings (she suspects, incidentally, that Polly has outbargained her in bidding for Macheath's favors); but the sweet naturalness of the music has brought out at the same time the genuine, even simple, intensity of her feeling: "his kiss was so sweet, and so closely he prest,/That I languish'd and pin'd 'till I granted the rest." The only alternative to knavery may be folly: "in love we are all fools alike"—but a fool may have a dignified simplicity. The mock-pastoral formula—having a barmaid sing an air of Purcell's—results in the tentative endorsement of a pastoral perception, that self-conscious, sophisticated calculation must yield to simple natural feeling, however "foolish."

Though Gay may have known the music in one of its numerous popular broadside versions, Lucy's song comes originally from the masque in Act III of Purcell's *Fairy Queen*. This "opera," or masque, or musical drama, is a shortened version of Shakespeare's *Midsummer Night's Dream*, with a masque inserted at the end of each act. The masque in Act III is designed to entertain Titania as she toys with Bottom in his translated, asinine form. Purcell's text for the song is apparently more simply innocent than Gay's: the soprano sings,

> If love's a sweet passion, why does it torment?
> If a bitter, oh tell me whence comes my content?
> Since I suffer with pleasure, why should I complain,
> Or grieve at my fate, when I know 'tis in vain?
> Yet so pleasing the pain is, so soft is the dart,
> That at once it both wounds me and tickles my heart.

The paradoxes are familiar; but the complications of Titania's situation gives them a satiric edge. The Queen of the Fairies is enamored of an ass; her love is not only pleasing and painful but complicated and simple, touching and comical, wise and foolish. Perhaps (especially if one thinks of Purcell's bawdy catches) the complications are sufficient to bring out the sexual significance of the conventional emblem: "so pleasing the pain is, so soft is the dart,/That at once it both wounds me and tickles my heart." In any case, the pastoral begins to mock itself, and continues to do so throughout the scene, not only in the texts of the songs, but in the amusing contrast of musical and literary styles, as fairies and savages, pastoral lovers and rustic haymakers successively divert themselves and the audience. If Gay's setting of the song stresses the mockery and Purcell's the pastoral, both recognize that pastoral must be capable of mocking itself if it is to be trusted.

The Beggar's Opera as Christian Satire

by Harold Gene Moss

While many artistic qualities of John Gay's *The Beggar's Opera* have proven attractive to one age after another—the delightful music, the comedy of the piece, the rapid wit of its dialogue (to name only a few) —reasons for its sustained appeal must be sought in some element of the opera that distinguishes it from the witty, comic, and musical works of Fielding, Lillo, and a host of their contemporaries whose appeal has been far less enduring. In fact, the unusually long life of Gay's opera arises essentially from the Christian myth expressed in Macheath and his environment, a myth that distinguishes the opera from its contemporary works, and lends it that substance by which masterpieces are known.

The history of the composition of *The Beggar's Opera* (January 1728) lends much important support to the notion that Gay was writing a satire based strictly on Christian values, one that compares with Alexander Pope's *Dunciad* (May 1728) and Jonathan Swift's *Gulliver's Travels* (1726), but such a reading of the work must derive from and be proven by the text itself.[1] In fact, the drama accumulates mythic energy through an essentially poetic process of increasingly dense patterns of allusion and imagery resulting in an allusive action that elevates Macheath during Act II to the stature of a cultural hero, a "supreme sacrificial hero" in the words of Professor William Empson. We are left at the work's end with "sympathetic terror," says Dr. John Aikin (a gifted physician and essayist writing in 1772), or with an "ultimate irony," in the words of Professor Bertrand Bronson.[2] In fact, we are left with the effects of a

---

"The Beggar's Opera *as Christian Satire*," by Harold Gene Moss. © *1975 by Harold Gene Moss. Used by permission of the author. This article appears for the first time in this volume.*

1 Historical support can be adduced from their mutual residence at Twickenham as Gay finished the opera. See Swift's letters in March and May, *The Correspondence of Jonathan Swift*, ed. Harold Williams, vol. iii (Oxford: Clarendon Press, 1963), pp. 246, 262, 278, 286.

2 Empson, *Some Versions of Pastoral* (London: Chatto & Windus, 1950), p. 230. Aikin, *Essays on Song-Writing* (London: Joseph Johnson, [1772]), p. 33. Bronson, "The Beggar's Opera," *Studies in the Comic* (Berkeley: University of California Press, 1941),

typically Augustan satire, the object of which is neatly summarized in the final verse paragraph of Gay's little-read poem "A Thought on Eternity":

> The virtuous soul pursues a nobler aim,
> And life regards but as a fleeting dream:
> She longs to wake, and wishes to get free,
> To launch from earth into eternity.[3]

The thesis developed in the following pages is that Gay represents life as a fleeting dream in *The Beggar's Opera,* a dream structured to satirize man's folly and vice from a timeless, Christian perspective.

The intellectual substance of *The Beggar's Opera* reveals itself most obviously in Gay's development of two major themes, love and time. A scene-by-scene examination of Acts I and II reveals that Gay prepares us carefully for the betrayal scene at the drama's center through foreshadowing and a progressive development of images and ideas. By the end of Act III, however, the moral opposition between Macheath and Peachum that exists through the major part of the work is purposefully destroyed by Gay along with the verisimilitude of his presentation—all of which turns the piece into a vastly ironic satire of contemporary life and taste. The principal action within the work relates overtly (as the betrayal scene) or covertly (as the prisoners' dance in chains) to Gay's orthodox belief in Christianity, a belief in large part identical to that of Pope and Swift.

From the first song of the opera, Gay emphasizes a distortion of the traditional views of love and order in society. What Swift observes so often in his sermons, Gay tells us with his first song: "Each neighbor abuses his brother" (Song 1), and, as both Swift and Pope show in their satires, man sinks to the level of the beast when traditional values are lost. Human life is valuable to Peachum only in terms of the money it will bring (I, ii). When Filch enters, Gay reveals another dimension of the society's twisted "love." His attachment to women is mechanically bestial, spiritually commercial: he impregnates them for a fee so they may "plead the belly" and avoid the gallows. Gay arranges for Filch to trace the origin of his immorality in the first song he sings: " 'Tis woman that seduces all mankind,/By her we first were taught the wheedling arts" (Song 2). At this moment Filch seems to understand that Betty Sly, who provided his "education," is only a latter-day Eve. At the next moment, he becomes a "messenger of comfort to friends in affliction," a kind of black angel

---

p. 230. All citation of *The Beggar's Opera* is to the edition by Professor Edgar V. Roberts (Lincoln: University of Nebraska Press, 1969). This essay was written with financial assistance from the Folger Shakespeare Library and the University of Florida.

[3] In *The Poetical Works of John Gay,* ed. John Underhill (London: Lawrence and Bullen, 1893), II, 244–46. The poem first appeared in Steele's *Miscellany* (1713) and was reprinted in the quarto edition of Gay's *Poems* (1720).

who takes Peachum's verdicts about life and death to prisoners waiting
at Newgate. Peachum tells us, "I *love* to make them easy one way or
another" (I, ii), an ultimately ironic use of the word "love" that reflects
back upon his command to Filch, "Let *my friends* know what I intend."
Peachum and Filch thus demonstrate vividly the current state of brotherly
love: men make beasts of themselves when they ignore Christian morality.

Gay's representation of love, even in these early pages of the opera,
obviously relates to the similar visions of it in Swift's and Pope's satires.
The world order controlled by Peachum is as morally perverted as that
dominated by the Goddess of Dullness or that asserted by Gulliver at
the close of his travels. In such satiric visions of the world, all the conventional symbols for social harmony are inverted and put to satiric use
by characters embodying evil. With manifold irony, Gay thus gives us
"a cordial for the time" (II, iii), a symbol of conviviality and communion
used by Macheath and his men to signal their love of life and also used
by Peachum, Lockit, Jenny Diver, and their followers as a mechanism
of betrayal.

The first time we see Macheath's men (II, i), they are drinking, await-
ing their leader and singing: "Fill ev'ry glass, for wine inspires us,/And
fires us/With courage, love and joy" (Song 19). Their burning inspiration, emphasized by the energetic musical setting, becomes a drive toward a way of life the very opposite of Peachum's. These men share an
emotional attachment to the pleasure of life, in contrast to Peachum and
his friends. As Nimming Ned asks, "Who is there here that would not
die for his friend?" (II, i), or, in the words of Ben Budge, "We are for a
just partition of the world, for every man hath a right to enjoy life."
Gay thus draws a contrast between the moral corruption of Peachum
and the fundamental virtue of Macheath's men in terms of their use of
cordials. As a traditional symbol of conviviality and a special symbol for
love in Pope and Rochester, the "Cordial Drop" signals for Macheath
and his men the genuine love that gives life.[4]

But just as the concept of love has been perverted by Peachum's influence, the "cordial of life" is associated with betrayal in his world. Twice
in Act I, as Gay exposes the corruption of the London underworld,
cordials are required by characters related to Peachum and, in each case,
they point to betrayal. First, Mrs. Peachum entices Filch to betray Polly
by telling what he knows of her affair with Macheath. "Come, Filch," she
says, "you shall go with me into my own room, and tell me the whole
story. I'll give thee a glass of a most delicious cordial that I keep for my

4 Background for the "cordial" as an image representing love can be found in
Pope's *Sixth Epistle of the First Book of Horace, Imitated* (1738), I, vi, 126–29, and
in Pope's source, the *Letter . . . from Artemisa . . . to Chloe* by John Wilmot, Earl
of Rochester (ll. 40–45) as quoted by Professor Butt in his edition of Pope's *Imitations
of Horace* (London: Methuen, 1939), vol. IV of the Twickenham Edition of Pope's
works.

own drinking" (I, vi). Filch's desire to remain loyal to Polly quickly gives way to the drink of seduction and betrayal. And later, when Polly admits that she married Macheath for love, not greed—understood by her parents as a betrayal of their trust in her—Mrs. Peachum swoons and Mr. Peachum commands her, "A glass of cordial, this instant" (I, viii). With this reversal of conventional imagery in the first act, Gay comments subtly on the morality of the Newgate environment and prepares us for the more important uses of the image later in the opera.

Having alerted us to the symbolism of the cordial and drinking and to the allusive action of his drama, Gay develops at the very center of the work (pp. 36–42 of an eighty-three-page edition) the most highly poetic scene of all, the betrayal of Macheath by Jenny Diver (II, iv). Macheath, etymologically "son of the heath" or "son of the earth," has called together a group of his followers for an evening's entertainment. The meeting is held under cover of darkness because the high priests of London crime have resolved to put him to death. As the scene progresses, we recognize, in fact, a ritualized enactment of betrayal. The group enjoys drink together—"Bid the drawer bring us more wine"—and they enjoy "the food of love." Each has an assigned seat at the master's table for what will be the last supper they have together: "Now, pray ladies, take your places," says the host, noting one of his followers in particular for her "sanctified look" and "mischievous heart": "You are not so fond of me, Jenny, as you used to be." She pretends special affection for Macheath only to relieve him of his pistols and to signal the waiting constables, saying, "I must and will have a kiss to give my wine a zest." Macheath is arrested and sings, as a parting comment, "At the tree I shall suffer with pleasure" (Song 25). Once he is gone, she offers the others "a bowl of punch or a treat," [5] a mock-communion service from which she absents herself.

Within the work's poetic and satiric structure, the scene becomes central to Gay's design. Jenny's signal to the constables refers both to the Judas-kiss of betrayal and to the inverted uses of the cordial and drinking images earlier in the work. The Christian virtues embodied in Macheath—his passionate love, his energetic support of life, his "innocent" regard for his fellow man—fall before the brutal, coldly rationalistic motives of Peachum, Lockit, and their tool, Jenny Diver. Thus the betrayal we witness in this scene, alluding broadly to the passion of Christ, is anticipated by the earlier action of the drama, the dominant allusions beneath the frothy surface of the play, and the key images Gay develops

---

[5] The word "treat" in certain rural English dialects means a loaf of bread made from the poorest of three qualities of flour. Nineteenth-century examples are recorded in the *O.E.D.* from the vicinity of Barnstaple where Gay spent his childhood and adolescence. Just as a "treat" is the cheapest of three kinds of bread, the "bowl of punch" Jenny offers is the cheapest of the three beverages mentioned in the *Opera* (wine, gin, and punch).

throughout. Just before this scene, Macheath makes one apparently casual remark that binds together the theme of love, the cordial images by which love is represented, and the theme of time: "I must have women," Macheath comments, "There is nothing unbends the mind like them. Money is not so strong *a cordial for the time*" (II, iii, italics mine). Indeed, Gay's management of theme and satire in the second half of the opera becomes apparent only when we trace the developing attitudes of his characters toward the human experience of time.

Frequently characters in the opera utter remarks about time that are the clichés of romance literature, the popular song, and the pastoral poem.[6] Filch's remark early in Act I, "Really, madam, I fear I shall be cut off in the flower of my youth" (I, vi), only initiates a series of similar clichés. When Macheath first sets foot upon the stage, he gives voice to another by asking Polly whether her love for him has not changed with the passage of time: "Did your fancy never stray/To some newer lover?" (Song 14). She turns the question back upon him, and he replies with Filch's metaphor:

> I sipped each flower,
> I changed ev'ry hour,
> But here [in you] ev'ry flower is united (Song 15).

The dramatic material and figurative statement are common to countless similar scenes in the drama, the love song, and the romance. But what happens next in the opera opens a new dimension to the subject. First, there are special pressures on the lovers' time. Polly says, "My papa and mamma are set against thy life. They *now, even now* are in search after thee. . . . *Thy life depends upon a moment*" (I, xiii, italics mine). Polly has been reading a romance lent her by Macheath (I, xiii), and her thoughts reflect it. But the dialogue begins to go beyond its origins into a language play entirely Gay's own. Here the word "depends" plays etymologically upon the idea of a physical object hanging from a point of suspension, the exact fate toward which Macheath moves in the drama. Thus Macheath's first conversation on stage focuses on time and serves to remind us that human life is frail: "Now, even now" death may come.

At the beginning of Act II Gay again brings up the subject of time in a context that demands special consideration. As the curtain rises Ben Budge asks: "But prithee, Matt, what is become of thy brother . . . ?" (II, i). Unlike Cain, Matt answers without hesitation: "He is among the ottomies [anatomies] at Surgeon's Hall." Ben replies, "So it seems his time was come," and Jemmy Twitcher adds, "But the present time is ours." The allusion to Genesis thus serves as a background for the comments made on time as well as for the demonstration of the human inclination to betray so fully developed in Act II. "What is become of thy

---

[6] I borrow a method and an emphasis from Empson's discussion of time, pp. 222–23.

brother?" becomes a central question in this part of the opera. "His time was come" is the only answer man can make.

With this the stage is set for the betrayal scene four pages later. In a world filled with deception and fraud, almost nothing endures the passage of time. As a character whose drives are toward love and the vital passions, Macheath becomes a Christ-like victim of the decadence surrounding him. Gay leaves us with the impression that the only human actions of enduring value are those which follow archetypal, hence timeless, patterns.

At the end of Act II, Gay develops further Macheath's character and along with it the religious meaning of his work. As they are about to part, Macheath encourages Lucy to haste by saying: "A moment of time may make us unhappy forever" (II, xv). Our first response to Gay's irony is that Macheath has simply reversed the seducer's cliché, *This moment of time, my dear, may make us happy forever*. Our second response, more consistent with Gay's handling of theme in the work, is: *A moment of evil in this life may damn us for an eternity*. Clearly the larger and more meaningful sense arises from the remark to parallel the traditional vision of human life in Gay's poem "A Thought on Eternity." In Act II, Gay thus surrounds Macheath with symbolic action and gives his words meaning that carries far beyond the dramatic context from which they arise. A climax of poetic intensity occurs with the betrayal scene because the foreshadowing has predicted this moment. Elevated to a heroic level by allusion and symbolic action, Macheath utters as the closing line of Act II a sentence that may be understood as a thesis statement for the entire opera: "A moment of time may make us unhappy forever." But let us look at Act III, where matters are not so clear, to discover what happens to Gay's satire and why the opera's intellectual basis has been so evasive.

As the curtain rises Lucy denies to her father that she helped Macheath to flee Newgate: "If I know anything of him I wish I may be burnt," she says, but her father wants another kind of martyrdom for her, not a gloriously romantic death by fire: "You shall fast and mortify yourself into reason, with now and then a little handsome discipline to bring you to your senses" (III, i). This ironically stated vision of man's aspiration toward divinity by martyrdom is to contrast with the bestiality of human life featured in the next scene, first in Lockit's assessment of the human species: "Lions, wolves, and vultures don't live together in herds, droves, or flocks. Of all animals of prey, man is the only sociable one. Every one of us preys upon his neighbor, and yet we herd together" (III, ii), and then in the language used in the exchange between Lockit and Filch. Lockit greets him, "Why, boy, thou lookest . . . like a shotten herring." Filch replies, "One need have the constitution of a horse to go through the business," the business being child-getting for a fee. Macheath then appears briefly, conversing with Ben Budge and Matt of the Mint in a gaming house (III, iv), a scene that serves only to remind us that the Captain is still at hand and may be apprehended again at any moment. The reminder soon takes shape when Diana Trapes gives Peachum and Lockit the information they need to find Macheath.

Next, and at some greater length, Gay contrasts Macheath's two "wives." With rationalistic and inhumane motives similar to those of her father, Lucy plots to poison Polly. The betrayal of friendship once again is associated with a cordial, the sham love that kills. Twice Lucy offers "ratsbane" to Polly, first in conversation, "in the way of friendship . . . [a] glass of cordial" (III, viii) and then in song,

> Come, sweet lass
> Let's take a chirping glass,
> Wine can clear
> The vapors of despair,
> And make us light as air . . . (Song 51).

The song is doubly ironic, first, because the "cordial" would indeed make Polly "light as air" and, second, because Gay's lyrics are set to the music of a popular love song and imitate in part its wording. The scene is interrupted by the reappearance of Macheath, guarded and ready for the gallows. The two daughters protest to their fathers but are denied in nicely symmetrical statements: "Macheath's time is come, Lucy," says Lockit, a remark that echoes Ben Budge's comment on the death of Matt's brother, "So it seems his time was come." Peachum's words for his daughter, "Set your heart at rest, Polly. Your husband is to die" (III, xi), similarly reflect back on the imagery related to the heart, the passions, and death. At this point all but two principal characters leave the stage, and a dance of prisoners in chains ensues.

Here Gay taunts us for a moment with the possibility that the opera may end with the dance. All the dramatic and poetic foreshadowing in the work points toward this moment as the opera's conclusion. We have seen how viciously this society destroys its members for profit, how omnipotently Peachum and Lockit control the London underworld, and how vulnerable Macheath is to their snares. We know that Lucy's stratagem to free him could work only once, and that no other escape is possible. "Macheath's time is come" is the only thought remaining as the action closes, and the dance is a fitting and usual concluding device at a play's end. Just as the dance of cuckolds at the end of Wycherley's *The Country Wife* reflects on the play's strange mixture of farce and satire, Gay's dance of prisoners would comment on the similar mixture of styles and meaning in his opera. The dancers' jangling movements mirror man's inability to achieve divine harmony. Their chains are the avarice and bestiality that entrap men in gross bodies and a corrupt society. And beyond this, Gay hints at a standard Christian emblem, the Dance of Death, making the scene additionally appropriate as a conclusion to what is thus far the plot of a Christian tragedy.

Of course Gay does not stop with the prisoners' dance. Instead he begins to break down for satiric reasons the verisimilitude of his drama and the initial coherence of its symbolic and moral contents. When the dance is done, Macheath appears in the condemned hold, apparently to face in solitude the final test of his values. He sings a series of ten songs without pause, a performance that is technically recitative, a feature of the Italian opera labeled "unnatural" by the Beggar in the framing scene at the opening of Gay's work. Ben and Matt once again enter and reveal to Macheath that Jemmy Twitcher, one of the trusted members of the gang, had in fact betrayed him to Lockit. Macheath's conclusion, " 'Tis a plain proof . . . that even our gang can no more trust one another than other people" (III, xiv), breaks down a part of the virtue earlier represented by Macheath and his men. The opposition between the two parties, Macheath's and Peachum's, thus dissolves, and with it goes the alignment of opposing characters upon which we had come to rely for the opera's moral message. The brotherly love of the gang and the cordial they drank to pledge it are now seen as false. Only moments later, a second part of Macheath's initial virtue fails when he causes Ben and Matt to swear that they will destroy Peachum and Lockit before they die: " 'Tis my last request. Bring those villains to the gallows" (III, xiv), making them the two thieves to be hanged inverted by the doomed Christ figure. Macheath's desire for revenge by death thus overwhelms the vitality he previously represented in the opera. But this shift in his characterization takes more definite form in the next scene when Macheath himself loses the "love of life" that previously animated his character. He protests twice in song, "See, my courage is out" (Song 68), as he tips up his empty bottle. Love, the "Cordial Drop" that "Heav'n in our cup has thrown," is now truly lost to Macheath. He tastes only "the nauseous Draught of Life," [7] the vicious and bestial pride that drives men toward death. When presented with the consequences of his earlier, vigorous love—four more wives, each with child in arms—he even pleads for death: "Here—tell the Sheriff's officers I am ready." This rejection of life marks the final deterioration of Macheath as a Christian protagonist. Faced with his final moments, the last test of a man's virtue, he breaks by succumbing to those drives represented initially by Peachum and Lockit. Hatred and death dominate his character at last. Gay very clearly shows us the final moment of transition from his former irrational vitality to his new state of mind when Macheath says: "Oh leave me to thought. I fear. I doubt" (Song 68). To end the scene, St. Sepulchre's

---

[7] Rochester's phrases; see ll. 43–45 of his *Letter.*

bell tolls and Macheath leaves for the gallows, guarded, chained, and broken.[8]

A second time, Gay taunts us with the possibility that the opera may end with Macheath's death. Verisimilitude demands such a conclusion, and the realistic texture of the work must be destroyed if he is to be saved. The Beggar and the Player, of course, intrude in the action, stop the hanging, and change Macheath's sentence from death to transportation. "All this we must do, to comply with the taste of the town" (III, xvi) is the Player's explanation for the reversal of action, an explanation that emerges after a brief debate between the two framing characters about the nature of the drama just witnessed. First, the Player objects to the hanging because it makes the work "a downright deep tragedy." The Beggar returns, "I was for doing strict poetical justice," a justice that demands Macheath's death. But in a manner similar to the struggle of the narrator of the *Dunciad* to maintain his artistic inspiration, Gay's Beggar (the nominal author of the opera) tries to keep poetic justice and the tragic sense originally intended for his work. And, just as the bad taste and dullness of society overwhelm Pope's narrator, the "taste of the town" overrides the Beggar's better judgment. Though none of the power and pathos of the *Dunciad's* conclusion are here, the similarity remains. By submitting to the taste of the town, the Beggar falls prey to those forces in contemporary society that Pope so violently attacked. The Beggar's final remark on the subject, "In this kind of drama 'tis no matter how absurdly things are brought about" (III, xvi), can be understood as a sweeping indictment of his own society: *In this kind of world 'tis no matter how absurdly art represents life.*

Macheath's final appearance on the stage, brief as it is, underscores two central themes in the opera and makes irrevocably clear the deterioration of his values. His song, set to the exotic tune of the bawdy "Lumps of Pudding," begins "Thus I stand like the Turk" (Song 69). Indeed he stands "like the Turk," stripped of the Christian values that he had evinced, as alien to the Christ-like figure of the betrayal scene as any heathen could be. The refrain of the song contains the second point: "The wretch of today may be happy tomorrow," says Macheath, a sentence repeated for emphasis by the chorus as the curtain descends at the opera's end. At first we think, *human life is wretched, but it may change.* From Macheath's point of view, a superior power has interrupted the

---

[8] The characterization of Macheath thus develops logically from *The Beggar's Opera* to *Polly*. His friendship with Jenny Diver, his inability to act with conviction and courage, and his willingness to betray his own men are all traits that confirm the moral deterioration of the character. Though *Polly* was not finished until December 1728 (published March 1729), Gay clearly had the plan of a sequel in mind when he has Macheath recommend the West Indies to Lucy and Polly as a place where they may begin new lives (*The Beggar's Opera*, III, xv).

normal course of life to produce an improvement in his world. But this ironic notion of an interposition of providence quickly gives way to a second response to the words: *The wretch of today may be happy tomorrow—or dead tomorrow,* the point being that man's finite intellect cannot ever know the future, not even from one moment to the next. And, of course, the remark begs to be compared to the similarly structured sentence that Macheath speaks at the end of Act II:

> *A moment of time* may make us unhappy *forever.*

The first is clearly Christian in its orientation. The tension is between a finite "time" and an infinite "forever," a tension that recalls Gay's handling of a religious world view in his poetry. But the second formulation substitutes for this tension indefinite references to moments of time, and the shift in meaning coincides exactly with the change in Macheath's morality. In the first statement, man's hope lies in good works, a life governed by brotherly love, and the life-sustaining irrationality of passion. In the second, man's hope lies in the chance of accidental good fortune, the kind of topsy-turvy luck that Macheath apparently thinks has saved him from the gallows. Gay leaves us with the impression that we have witnessed the deterioration of an ultimate human virtue, that represented by Macheath and that embodied by the dramatic art itself. As Macheath changes from a mythic hero to a satiric knave, so the Beggar changes from the poet who writes truth to one who serves the taste of the town. Without principles, "like the Turk," Macheath is celebrated by the Beggar. The chaos of time changes all things human, both the embodiment of virtue and the poetic vision by which it is understood.

The Beggar's Opera is not a tragedy. But in many ways it functions with respect to tragedy as the *Dunciad* does with respect to the epic poem. Both authors work their materials against the background of a higher style, both develop extensive allusions to Christian materials that fall into an orderly satirical scheme, and from both works arises an enduring sense of human frailty when man and society are tested by absolute Christian standards. The occasional satire on the surface of both works attracted and held the attention of eighteenth-century critics, but close examination reveals that the satires in fact remain interesting and moving to one generation of readers after another because they are deeply rooted in the traditions of Western culture, particularly those Christian values expressed by Swift in his sermon "On Brotherly Love," by Pope in *The Essay on Man,* and by Gay in his "A Thought on Eternity." Irrational inspiration and irrational vitality are traces of the divine spark in man, but these traits may be destroyed by man's cold rationality, his depravity, and his propensity to commit sin.

"A Double Capacity": *The Beggar's Opera*

by Ian Donaldson

For the generality of men, a true Modern Life is like a true
Modern Play, neither Tragedy, Comedy, nor Farce, nor one, nor
all of these. Every Actor is much better known by his having
the same Face, than by his keeping the same Character: For
we change our minds as often as they can their parts, & he who
was yesterday Cesar, is to day Sir J. Daw. So that one might,
with much better reason, ask the same Question of a Modern
Life, that Mr. Rich did of a Modern Play; Pray do me the
favor, Sir, to inform me: Is this your Tragedy or your Comedy?

Pope to Cromwell, 29 August 1709 [1]

I

The Beggar's Opera has had a remarkable stage history, in respect both
of its enduring popularity and of the wide variety of ways in which it
has been interpreted. Its popularity in modern times derives very largely
from two famous and quite different productions of the 1920s. Nigel
Playfair's long-running London production (which in turn set off a train
of critical and scholarly works and small editions of the plays) was pretty
and porcelain, its music (arranged by Frederick Austen) decorative, sweet,
pathetic. Bertolt Brecht's adaptation, *Die Dreigroschenoper,* presented
in Berlin in 1928, was quite another thing, its caustically unsentimental
tone perfectly conveyed by the music of Kurt Weil. Neither production
could be said to have interpreted *The Beggar's Opera* very faithfully,
and it is understandable that Empson should have spoken tartly in his
splendid essay on the play in the early thirties: "It is a fine thing that
the play is still popular, however stupidly it is enjoyed." [2] And yet there
has seldom been a period in which *The Beggar's Opera* has not been, in
some sense, "stupidly" enjoyed, and this tendency to provoke a wide
range of responses and interpretations is not the least intriguing aspect

---

1 *The Correspondence of Alexander Pope,* ed. George Sherburn (Oxford, 1956), i. 71.
2 William Empson, *'The Beggar's Opera,'* in *Some Versions of Pastoral* (2nd imp.,
London, 1950), p. 250.

of the play. Eighteenth-century performances of the play were quite as
various as those in modern times. In 1777—to take just one instance—
The Whitehall Evening Post found occasion to complain with equal tart-
ness of the two productions of *The Beggar's Opera* then running at the
two main London theatres; at one house Lucy was being played as high
tragedy, at the other she was played as low comedy, and "we scruple not
to pronounce them both wrong." [3] Not tragedy, not comedy; then what
do you call it? In an earlier rehearsal play, Gay had put that question
in his very title: *The What D'Ye Call It.* The play defied all categories;
it was, said Gay, "A Tragi-Comi-Pastoral Farce." There is a well-known
letter in which Pope and Gay speak delightedly of the bewildering effect
The What D'Ye Call It has had upon its audiences. Some of the town,
they write, have taken the play as "a mere jest upon the tragic poets,"
others have seen it as a satire on the late war; the deaf Mr. Cromwell,
hearing none of the words, was much surprised to see the audience laughing at such apparently tragical action; those who came to hiss were so
diverted that they forgot the purpose of their visit. The "common people
of the pit and gallery," Pope and Gay go on, "received it at first with
great gravity and sedateness, some few with tears; but after the third
day they also took the hint, and have ever since been loud in their
clapps." [4] It was a perfect Scriblerian victory; a victory for what Hugh
Kenner has well described as the art of counterfeiting.[5] Counterfeiting is
quite different from hoaxing; the puzzlement set up by *The What D'Ye
Call It* or *The Beggar's Opera* is of quite a different order from that
temporary puzzlement aroused by, let us say, Ireland's *Vortigern.* Even
after long familiarity with Gay's work, even after taking "the hint," one
is still likely to feel the variousness of its appeal, its odd ability to be at
once ironical and sentimental, risible and grave.

A small cross-section taken from near the end of *The Beggar's Opera*
will show how Gay's kind of counterfeiting works, and how complex its
effects may be. A writer in the first number of *The Sentimental Magazine*
in 1773 observed that the principal difficulty of approaching Gay's work
was to know how seriously it was intended, as simplicity and "the real
pathetic" are so intermingled with the humorous and parodic that "one
is at loss whether to take it as jest or earnest—whether to laugh or cry."
"Indeed," he went on, after discussing this difficulty in relation to *The
Shepherd's Week,*

> this effect is also produced in his two dramatic burlesques, the Beggar's
> Opera and What d'ye call it; for how ludicrous soever the general char-
> acter of the piece may be, when he comes so near to hanging and shooting

3 *The Whitehall Evening Post,* Tuesday, November 11, 1777; cited in W. E. Schultz,
Gay's 'Beggar's Opera' (New Haven and London, 1923), pp. 76–77.
4 *The Letters of John Gay,* ed. C. F. Burgess (Oxford, 1966), p. 19 (letter of March 3,
1714/15).
5 Hugh Kenner, *The Counterfeiters* (Bloomington and London, 1968).

[*sic*] in good earnest, the joke ceases; and I have observed the tolling of
St. *Pulcre's-bell* received by an audience with as much tragical attention
and sympathetic terror as that in Venice Preserved.

The testimony about eighteenth-century audience reaction to the final
moments of *The Beggar's Opera* is of some interest; so too is the fact that
the writer should turn instinctively for his comparison to a similar effect
in Otway's *Venice Preserv'd*. For it seems highly probable that Otway's
scene was just the one which Gay here intended to burlesque. Pierre's
heroic ascent to the scaffold in Act v of *Venice Preserv'd* was one of the
most celebrated tragic moments of the Restoration and eighteenth-century stage. As Pierre awaits his execution, the *Passing-bell tolls*; assured
by his friend Jaffeir that his death will be honourable—Jaffeir will stab
him, then stab himself, at the gallows—Pierre proudly presents himself
to his executioners with the measured words, *Come, now I'm ready*. That
bell had been gently mocked by Addison in the forty-fourth *Spectator*
paper as early as 1711; and the year after the first performance of *The
Beggar's Opera* Pope was also to speak dryly of the tolling bell as "a
mechanical help to the Pathetic, not unuseful to the modern writers of
Tragedy." [6] Gay's use of the tolling bell in the last act of *The Beggar's
Opera* as Macheath, standing between Polly and Lucy, also awaits Jack
Ketch ("Would I might be hanged!") just as clearly mocks this highly
popular dramatic device. Suddenly confronted with four more wives, with
a child apiece, Macheath reaches desperately for the dignity of Pierre's
own phrase: *"Here—tell the Sheriffs officers I am ready."* (An extra relish
was given to the allusion by the fact that Walker, the actor playing Macheath in the original production at Lincoln's Inn Fields, had also played
Pierre at the same theatre a few weeks earlier.)[7] No gallows joke, I suppose, is likely to be simple in its effects; that this one should compel an
audience to "tragical attention and sympathetic terror" does suggest,
however, an abnormal emotional complexity, an abnormal success at
the counterfeiter's art. "Sublimity," wrote Goldsmith, "if carried to an
exalted height, approaches burlesque. . . ." [8] Gay's art reverses the
process: his burlesque, carried to an exalted height, approaches sublimity.

Gay's counterfeiting is different not only from mere hoaxing but also
from mere literary parody and ridicule. His style of burlesque is quite
unlike that of Buckingham. "Our Poets make us laugh at Tragoedy / And
with their Comedies they make us cry," Buckingham had written in the
prologue to *The Rehearsal*, stating what was to become the commonest
of eighteenth-century theatrical jokes, that it was impossible nowadays
to tell comedy and tragedy apart. Behind this joke lay the neo-classical

6 *The Dunciad* (1729), ii. 220 n.
7 *The London Stage, 1660–1800*, ed. Emmett L. Avery; Part 2: *1700–29* (Carbondale,
Illinois, 1960), p. 950.
8 'An Enquiry into the Present State of Polite Learning in Europe,' in *The Collected
Works of Oliver Goldsmith*, ed. Arthur Friedman (Oxford, 1966), i. 288.

premiss that comedy and tragedy ought to be firmly kept apart; the premiss of Goldsmith's *Essay on the Theatre,* in which he complains that comedy and tragedy, traditionally kept in "different channels," had lately encroached upon each other's provinces. Gay converts a stock joke into a new art-form. *"The whole Art of* Tragi-Comi-Pastoral Farce," he wrote in his Preface to *The What D'Ye Call It, "lies in interweaving the several kinds of the Drama with each other, so that they cannot be distinguished or separated."* And in his "interweaving" of the dramatic kinds Gay gently challenges the old neo-classical premiss that insists that the kinds be kept pure and distinct. In *The Beggar's Opera* heroic tragedy, Italian opera, pastoral, popular ballads, and sentimental comedy merge bizarrely together, continually awakening ironical memories of other kinds of literary experience yet nevertheless forming a whole which is in some ways curiously life-like. "By the assumed licence of the mock-heroic style," Hazlitt wrote perceptively, Gay "has enabled himself to *do justice to nature."* [9] What is "natural," perhaps, is the sense which Gay stimulates of the manifold possible ways of looking at any set of actions: as in life itself, an act may be heroic, or laughable, or sad; the plays are unclassifiable, open-ended. And in this respect they may strike us as being peculiarly modern.

The challenge to neo-classical principles was also being made about this time by other and more serious campaigners. Steele had argued in *Tatler* 172 that one really ought to be able to write tragedy not only about "the history of princes, and persons who act in high spheres," but also about "such adventures as befall persons not elevated above the common level." The common man is potentially as much of a tragic figure as is the prince. It is little wonder that eighteenth-century audiences were confused as to the proper way of responding to the echoes of *Venice Preserv'd* as Macheath went to the gallows at the end of *The Beggar's Opera,* for such echoes of heroic tragedy were a common device in the new bourgeois tragedy. Only three years after the first performance of *The Beggar's Opera,* George Lillo in the final act of *The London Merchant* was to imitate closely the final act of *Venice Preserv'd*: as George Barnwell awaits his execution at the scaffold, the passing bell tolls once more, and Barnwell, like Macheath, prepares to meet his death with a half-quotation from Otway on his lips: "I am summoned to my fate. . . . *Tell 'em I'm ready."* The fate of a London prentice, Lillo implies, should hold the same poignancy for us as the fate of Macbeth or Faustus or Pierre. If a prentice may take on heroic stature, why may not a highwayman too? In his Preface to *The What D'Ye Call It* Gay had gravely repeated the arguments of the propagandists for the new bourgeois tragedy. To the "objection" that the sentiments of the play

9 *The Complete Works of William Hazlitt,* ed. P. P. Howe, after the edition of A. R. Waller and Arnold Glover (London and Toronto, 1930), iv. 65.

are *"not Tragical, because they are those of the lowest country people,"* he answered:

> *". . . that the sentiments of Princes and clowns have not in reality that difference which they seem to have: their thoughts are almost the same, and they only differ as the same thought is attended with a meanness or pomp of diction, or receive a different light from the circumstances each Character is conversant with."*

Gay puts a new ironical edge on the sentimentalists' proposition. It is only "circumstances" and the artificial conventions of "diction" (high style for princes, low style for clowns) which disguise the basic truth that all men are alike, that those in low life are no worse than those in high, that those in high life are no better than those in low. All men may therefore be seen as heroes; or, if you prefer, all men may therefore be seen as rogues. And so often in Gay's work, the question is left open: we may look at it which way we please. Yet what we cannot forget—and the fact is important to an understanding of *The Beggar's Opera*—is the general sense of the interchangeability of men. Despite all appearances, one man will turn out to be much the same as another.

II

The Beggar's Opera, wrote Pope, was "a piece of Satire which hit all tastes and degrees of men, from those of the highest Quality to the very Rabble." [10] All classes and all men come within the arc of its satire; no one is left unscathed. Yet it is the method of Gay's irony to keep maintaining the illusion that this is not so at all; that although things are in a bad way in this society there must surely be exceptions somewhere to the general rule; someone must be kind, someone must be honest, someone must be heroic. Throughout the play Gay keeps suggesting possible exceptions to the general rule of bourgeois possessiveness and self-interest, possible avenues of romantic freedom and escape, possible evidence of a primitive honestry; only regretfully, ironically, to dismiss such possibilities, to shut off the avenues and to reject the evidence as we approach more nearly.

The method is seen at its broadest in the opening song of the play:

> Through all the employments of life
>   Each neighbour abuses his brother;
> Whore and Rogue they call Husband and Wife:
>   All professions be-rogue one another.
> The Priest calls the Lawyer a cheat,
>   The lawyer be-knaves the Divine;
> And the Statesman, because he's so great,
>   Thinks his trade as honest as mine.

10 *The Dunciad* (1729), iii. 326 n.

Peachum's song pictures a society in which all men are reduced to a common level: husbands and wives stand on the same footing as rogues and whores; priests and lawyers are as bad as each other; all men are "brothers" in that they are all united in knavery. Yet there is one exception to this cheerless general rule, one honest man in this corrupt society: Peachum. And Peachum's "trade" is that of an informer and receiver of stolen goods. Peachum explains how his trade might be said to be honest: "A Lawyer is an honest employment, so is mine. Like me too he acts in a double capacity, both against Rogues and for 'em; for 'tis but fitting that we should protect and encourage Cheats, since we live by 'em." "A double capacity," Peachum implies, is twice as useful as a single one; the phrase suggests a sophisticated professional versatility, like that of the lawyer, who can now prosecute, now defend, using the law as a rapier or as a shield as the need arises. No one needs to be told that Peachum's "capacity" is in fact that of the double agent, that he is as great a rogue as everyone else in his society. The phrase "double capacity" might also be said to describe the way in which Gay's own irony works, saying one thing and implying another, shaping a double picture of Peachum and (in turn) of every other character in the play.

The ironical method in this opening passage is enjoyably broad and easy; no one could be fooled by Peachum. Yet it is worth watching even at this stage of the play how Gay creates an awareness that things may be seen in a multiplicity of ways. Here is how Peachum resolves to secure the release from Newgate of some female members of the gang: "I love to let the women scape. A good sportsman always lets the Hen-Partridges fly, because the breed of the game depends upon them. Besides, here the Law allows us no reward; there is nothing to be got by the death of women—except our wives." Sportsman's heartiness, old-fashioned gallantry to the ladies, and financial shrewdness are nicely blended. The passage invites us to see Peachum as soft-hearted, and to see him as callous; to see women as objects of chivalry, and to see them as mere "game"; to see them as being of value, because they are breeders, and as being of no value, for the law allows no reward for information against them. Everything depends upon your viewpoint. Like hen-partridges the women are allowed to escape, but like hen-partridges they are at the same time captive within the lord's domain; the image of the bird which is apparently free but in fact captive runs throughout the play. Then the perspective shifts once more; women are praised, in a barbed phrase, as the educators of men and their rewarders ("We and the surgeons are more beholden to women than all the professions beside"), then instantly condemned as the seducers of men:

> 'Tis woman that seduces all mankind,
>   By her we first were taught the wheedling arts:
> Her very eyes can cheat; when most she's kind,
>   She tricks us of our money with our hearts.

> For her, like Wolves by night we roam for prey,
> And practise ev'ry fraud to bribe her charms;
> For suits of love, like law, are won by pay,
> And Beauty must be fee'd into our arms.

It is not the men who trap the women—thus runs the argument of Filch's song—but rather the women who trap the men, as they have done since the time of Eve, the archetypal wheedler and betrayer. The men are betrayed by the softness of their hearts. The betrayal is not that the women are unfaithful, but that they demand cash. Hence men are turned into predatory *"Wolves,"* against their better natures. What should be noticed is the revolution of images here, as men and women take it in turns to be hungry predators and innocent victims, wolves and partridges, confusing in our minds the notion of who is hunting whom, but suggesting obliquely that everyone may be seen as acting in a double capacity, that no one is simply a hunter or simply a prey, that society is at war with itself, and that that war is at its most deadly in the relationship between the sexes. Tempering such suggestions is the gaiety of the dramatic moment; the predominant mood is set by the light, darting melody to which the song is set. The final effect is thus one of incongruity: the incongruity of a sharpster protesting that he had been undone, yet at the same time educated, by the ladies; the incongruity of words and music, as this unsettling vision of society is unfolded with such gay charm.

This ironic revolution of images continues throughout the play; it is typical of Gay's method that within one song (Air XLV) he should have Lockit picturing himself first as a gudgeon, the "easy prey" of his treacherous daughter, next as a trapper, catching one innocent bird (Macheath) with another unwitting decoy (Lucy). It is in the case of Macheath and Polly that this confusion of role is most delicately suggested; and once again the predominant images are those of hunter and hunted. Mrs. Peachum's wish is to save Macheath from the predatory company of lords and gentlemen; "he should leave them to prey upon one another." Yet it is more logical (as Samuel Butler had suggested) to see a highwayman himself as an animal of prey: "Aristotle held him to be but a kind of huntsman; but our sages of the law account him rather a beast of prey, and will not allow his game to be legal by the forest law." [11] We are to learn in due course (III. ii) that the image is an apt one for Macheath, who keeps company with lords and gentlemen in their gaming-houses merely so as to know who is worth setting upon on the road. And yet (as Empson's analysis makes clear) there is also the suggestion that Macheath may indeed be a victim, in his relationship with Polly:

[11] Samuel Butler, *Characters and Passages from Note-Books,* ed. A. R. Waller (Cambridge, 1908), p. 227.

I know as well as any of the fine ladies [says Polly] how to make the most of my self and of my man too. A woman knows how to be mercenary, though she hath never been in a court or at an assembly. We have it in our natures, papa. If I allow captain *Macheath* some trifling liberties, I have this watch and other visible marks of his favour to show for it.

For a new wife to claim that she knows how "to make the most" of her husband suggests that she has a concern for advancing him in the world. What Polly has in fact been doing (the syntax glides us demurely over the point) is getting what she can out of her husband in order to line her own pockets.

The imagery of Polly's songs continues the doubt as to who is hunting whom:

> I, like a ship in storms, was tost;
> Yet afraid to put in to Land;
> For seiz'd in the port the vessel's lost,
> Whose treasure is contreband.
>   The Waves are laid,
>   My duty's paid.
> O joy beyond expression!
>   Thus, safe a-shore,
>   I ask no more,
> My all is in my possession.

"Duty" is both a tax, and a moral obligation; the word chimes ironically throughout the play. For other characters than Polly, it seems, "duty" is something one owes to oneself, and is closely connected with the idea of self-interest. "If she will not know her duty," says her mother, "we know ours"; the duty is to hang Macheath before he hangs them. For the ladies of the town, love is the "duty" which they owe to themselves in their youth (Air XXII); the gang go "upon duty" on the heath in order to make themselves rich. Polly's duty, on the other hand, appears to be directed outwards; there seems to be something endearingly old-fashioned about her ideas of social responsibility. And yet the song also pictures Polly as a smuggler; the contraband "treasure" is Macheath (Gay has given a specific sense to the colloquial phrase, "you treasure"), who is reduced to a mere possession which Polly is now free to enjoy. She is free, Macheath is a mere possession; the highwayman, whose job it is to capture other people's treasure, is himself captured by Pirate Polly. The point is again made with a sweet obliqueness (quite lost in Brecht's "Pirate Jenny"), the whole conceit of the song apparently arising out of an innocent imitation of a favourite operatic simile ("the ship") which the Beggar has warned us earlier he will introduce by way of heightening. The adventurer and the turtle-dove; such is Polly's double capacity.

It is this controlled confusion of imagery which causes, in turn, our confusion of response as we watch the play. It is perhaps as important that the sentimentality of the play can hold the irony in check as it is the other way about; Brecht's version of the play shows how much is lost by the removal of this sentimental counterweight. There is nothing in *Die Dreigroschenoper* which manages to strike a note quite like this:

> Now I'm a wretch indeed—Methinks I see him already in the cart, sweeter and more lovely than the nosegay in his hand!—I hear the crowd extolling his resolution and intrepidity!—What vollies of sighs are sent from the windows of *Holborn,* that so comely a youth should be brought to disgrace!—I see him at the tree! the whole Circle are in tears!—even Butchers weep!—*Jack Ketch* himself hesitates to perform his duty, and would be glad to lose his fee, by a reprieve.

In 1770 Francis Gentleman, writing in *The Dramatic Censor,* praised this speech for its pathos and simplicity: ". . . the breaks are fine, the sentiments tender, the description lively, all dressed in a naïveté of language, which finds a passage to the heart, by nature's aid alone." [12] Gay's counterfeiting is such that it is possible to believe that one is watching an orthodox sentimental drama. "Those cursed Play-books she reads have been her ruin," Mrs. Peachum has said of her daughter, and Polly's speech is a creditable imitation of the way in which the heroines of the play-books deliver themselves. Polly sees life as like a play, and the assumption that underlies her speech is that in real life people will behave as they do in theatres: "the whole Circle are in tears," butchers will weep and hangmen melt, everyone will wish for a happy ending. Yet this *is* a play which we are watching, and Macheath *will* be saved (just as Polly hopes) by a reprieve; hence for those (like Francis Gentleman) used to the sentimental traditions, the speech seems to work "by nature's aid alone."

Though Gentleman was quick enough to spot particular touches of literary parody throughout the play, he was evidently prepared to regard certain whole scenes as genuinely pathetic. The first encounter between Polly and Macheath he seemed to regard in this light. "His reluctance to fly, and her tender resolution to part for a time rather than hazard his safety," he ventured, "raise delicate feelings." [13] This scene is, of course, partly intended to ridicule the hackneyed stock scenes of parting lovers, but there is some kind of justification for Gentleman's remarks: certainly the parody is not forced upon us in the way it had been in Cibber's *The Comical Lovers* or as it was to be in the equally ludicrous parting scene in Sheridan's *The Critic.* Such concealment of the parodic tactics heightens the whole scene between Polly and Macheath. *"Were I laid on Greenland's coast"* pictures an idyllic lovers' escape, in the style of "Come live with me and be my love" or "If you were the only girl in the world," but is actually—as Empson pointed out—a reply to a question about

---

[12] *The Dramatic Censor* (London, 1770), i. 117. The passage was also admired by Hazlitt: ibid. iv. 65.
[13] *The Dramatic Censor,* i. 117–18.

transportation. And at least some members of the audience must have recalled the last time they had heard that tune on stage, in Farquhar's *The Recruiting Officer*, where both words and context were very different; what Kite and his recruits were celebrating there was their proposed escape from the very domestic ties in which Macheath is now entangling himself:

> We all shall lead more happy lives
> By getting rid of brats and wives,
> That scold and brawl both night and day—
> Over the hills and far away.

The total effect is—as Boswell remarked of another song earlier in the play—"at once . . . painful and ridiculous." [14]

Throughout the play each character in turn speaks kindly about his *heart*. Peachum finds that "it grieves one's heart to take off a great man"; and Mrs. Peachum pleads with him that he be, like herself, not "too hard-hearted." Polly's heart, she tells us at once, yields very readily:

> Though my heart were as frozen as Ice,
> At his flame 'twould have melted away.

And throughout the play Polly's heart, like Lucy's, contrives to melt, bleed, split, burst, and break; "I know my heart," she modestly remarks. Macheath in his first song announces that "My heart was so free," but now it is "riveted" to Polly's; before long, Macheath is in search of the "free-hearted ladies" of the town. The variation in the depth of the irony means that some of these claims to free- or tender-heartedness are likely to win a temporary credibility. But we can never quite forget the talk of *double capacity* with which the play began; people are likely to play more roles than one; soft hearts may turn to hard; the man who professes himself the lovable victim of society may turn out to be a predator and oppressor. The second act opens with a new mirage of the free life, created by Macheath's gang. Like everyone else, the gang speak well of their hearts: money "was made for the free-hearted and generous, and where is the injury of taking from another, what he hath not the heart to make use of?" Here is their apologia for the highwayman's profession:

> *Jemmy Twitcher* . . . Why are the laws levell'd at us? are we more dishonest than the rest of mankind? what we win, gentlemen, is our own by the law of arms, and the right of conquest.
> *Crook-finger'd Jack.* Where shall we find such another set of practical philosophers; who to a man are above the fear of Death?
> *Wat Dreary.* Sound men, and true!
> *Robin of Bagshot.* Of try'd courage, and indefatigable industry!
> *Nimming Ned.* Who is there here that would not dye for his friend?

14 *Boswell's Life of Johnson*, ed. G. B. Hill, rev. L. F. Powell (Oxford, 1934), ii. 368.

Harry Padington. Who is there here that would betray him for his interest?
Matt of the Mint. Show me a gang of Courtiers that can say as much.
Ben Budge. We are for a just partition of the world, for every man hath a
right to enjoy life.
Matt. We retrench the superfluities of mankind. The world is avaricious, and
I hate avarice.

This variant of the levellers' plea—beginning with the claim "we're no
worse than our betters," and edging quickly to the larger one, "we're
better than our betters"—has an interesting contemporary analogue:
namely, the formal apologias for the merchant's profession commonly
found in the new middle-class drama of the day. Steele's Mr. Sealand in
The Conscious Lovers (IV. ii), and Gay's own Mr. Barter in *The Distress'd
Wife* (IV. xvi), champion the merchants against their "betters," the landed
gentry, in very similar style; Lillo's Thorowgood and Trueman in *The
London Merchant* were likewise soon to present a panegyric of the merchant as one who relieves nations of their "useless superfluities," deliver-
ing them to other nations in need (III. i). As the merchants justify their
occupation, so with equal reasonableness the gang justify theirs. Their
defence is attractive, just as Polly's pathos is attractive; and, like Polly,
the gang win their admirers: one modern critic seems prepared to take
them at their word, considering the passage to represent Gay's own views
on the desirability of the even distribution of wealth throughout society.[15]
Yet it is impossible to forget both the context of the passage and the
whole ironical movement of the play. For all their fine free-heartedness,
for all their Robin Hood air of disinterested charity, the gang acts, as
everyone else does, in a double capacity. For Macheath, friendship is
nowhere to be found save with the gang:

> The modes of the Court so common are grown,
> That a true friend can hardly be met;
> Friendship for interest is but a loan,
> Which they let out for what they can get.

Corruption has spread outwards from the Court to infect all society;
"interest"—a complex word of the time, signifying both financial interest and self-interest of the kind spoken of by Hobbes[16]—rules everywhere. But Macheath clings to the one exception to the general rule:
"But we, gentlemen, have still honour enough to break through the
corruptions of the world." Yet, to Macheath's astonishment, it is finally
a member of the gang, Jemmy Twitcher, who betrays him—"a plain
proof that the world is all alike, and that even our Gang can no more
trust one another than other people." Locke in his *Essay Concerning*

15 Sven M. Armens, *John Gay, Social Critic* (New York, 1954), p. 56.
16 For a discussion of some contemporary usages of the word see Felix Raab, *The
English Face of Machiavelli* (London and Toronto, 1964), pp. 157–68.

Human Understanding (Bk. 1, Ch. 2, § 2), discussing whether or not there could be said to exist any innate moral principles, had interested himself particularly in the moral code of highway men. "Justice and truth are the common ties of society; and therefore even outlaws and robbers, who break with all the world besides, must keep faith and rules of equity amongst themselves; or else they cannot hold together." [17] Finally Macheath's gang are shown to lack even that faith and those rules of equity; like everyone else, they are governed solely by "interest."

Behind the charm and sentiment of the play is a Hobbesian vision of a world dominated by universal interest. And it is with Hobbes in mind that we should look at the play's central cluster of images, those which compare and contrast human and animal life. Throughout both his dramatic and his non-dramatic work Gay continually glances back and forth between the world of men and the world of beasts, implying continually that that of the beasts is preferable to that of men:

> But is not man to man a prey?
> Beasts kill for hunger, man for pay.
> (Fable X)

> Here *Shock*, the pride of all his kind, is laid;
> Who fawn'd like Man, but n'er like Man betray'd.
> ("Elegy on a Lap-Dog")

This contrast (as we noticed in Chapter Five)[18] is thoroughly traditional to both pastoral and satire, yet in *The Beggar's Opera* it appears to take on a specific coloration from a still-current philosophical debate. Lockit's speech in the third act of the play should be the starting-point here: "Lions, Wolves, and Vultures don't live together in herds, droves, or flocks.—Of all animals of prey, man is the only sociable one. Every one of us preys upon his neighbour, and yet we herd together." The background of this well-known speech is worth investigating.

Up until about the middle of the seventeenth century one of the popular "proofs" of God's benign ordering of the universe was the fact that animals of prey hunted alone or in pairs, while grazing animals and those necessary to man's comfort and well-being grouped themselves together conveniently in herds. Were the predators to move about in herds, remarked Henry Peacham (the author of *The Compleat Gentleman*) in mild alarm in 1622, "they would undo a whole country." [19] This "proof" about the habits of herding animals and solitary animals was

17 *An Essay Concerning Human Understanding*, ed. A. C. Fraser (Oxford, 1894).

18 George Boas, *The Happy Beast in French Thought of the Seventeenth Century* (Baltimore, 1933). Cf. Wycherley's poem '*Upon the Impertinence of* Knowledge, *the Unreasonableness of* Reason, *and the Brutality of* Humanity; *proving the Animal Life the most Reasonable Life, since the most Natural, and most Innocent,*' in *The Complete Works of William Wycherley,* ed. Montague Summers (London, 1924), iii. 149–54.

19 Henry Peacham, *The Compleat Gentleman,* ed. Virgil B. Heltzel (New York, 1962), p. 79.

adduced to support a generally optimistic theory about the efficient organization of the human and animal kingdoms, and of the relationship between them. It was a natural corollary of this theory that human beings themselves, who came together in "herds" to form towns and cities, were to be reckoned more like cows than like wolves, being pacific rather than warlike. Aristotle had put this even more flatteringly: like ants and bees, men come together naturally and for the common good, yet they are by nature superior to those creatures, because of their knowledge of language, of justice, of good and evil.[20] This theory was devastated by Hobbes at the middle of the century. Men do not come naturally together for the common good (Hobbes argued), but rather for a variety of selfish reasons: for honour, dignity, passion, glory, gain. Man is more like a wolf than he is like a cow or a bee. The human community is unique in that it is the only "herd" which is composed of animals of prey: therefore its laws and government must be powerfully devised and powerfully imposed.[21] Shaftesbury in his various replies to Hobbes tried to attack this proposition; in his "An Inquiry Concerning Virture or Merit" in 1699 he refined the old argument about wild animals living on their own and tame ones sheltering together, and in *Sensus Communis:* "An Essay on the Freedom of Wit and Humour" in 1709 he insisted upon the naturalness and the mutual usefulness and pleasure of human herding: "If eating and drinking be natural," he wrote, "herding is so too. If any appetite or sense be natural, the sense of fellowship is the same." [22]

Two distinct views of man as a "sociable animal" were therefore current at the time at which Gay wrote *The Beggar's Opera*: the sceptical Hobbesian view, and the more optimistic view of Shaftesbury, which argued that sociability, like the other human passions, was both instinctive and conducive to the common good; that self-interest and social interest might be the same. There is little doubt, I think, that the Hobbesian view pervades *The Beggar's Opera*; but Gay's achievement is to throw up as an ironical alternative the sentimental Shaftesburian view of things, appearing, as it were, to weigh the two socia˙ theories judiciously in the balance, hinting that there *might* be exceptions to the general Hobbesian rule. The Peachums and Lockits, the lords and the gamesters of London come together as Hobbes reckoned men always did in cities, out of self-interest and a desire for mutual plunder. "If you would not be look'd upon as a fool," says Lockit to his daughter, "you should never do anything but upon the foot of interest. Those that act otherwise are their own bubbles." The gamesters are

---

[20] Aristotle, *Politics*, ed. Ernest Barker (Oxford, 1946), I. ii, § 10 (pp. 5–6).
[21] See especially *De Cive*, II. v, § 5; *Leviathan*, ii. 17.
[22] Shaftesbury, 'An Inquiry Concerning Virtue or Merit,' in *Characteristics*, ed. John W. Robertson (London, 1900), i. 237–338; '*Sensus Communis:* An Essay on the Freedom of Wit and Humour,' in *Characteristics*, i. 74.

Like pikes, lank with hunger, who miss of their ends,
They bite their companions and prey on their friends.

"Man is a herded animal, and made for Towns and Cities," says one
of the characters in Shadwell's *Bury Fair*; and Gay's vision of the city
is the same Hobbesian vision as Shadwell had presented in that play:
"So many Pens of Wild Beasts upon two legs, undermining, lying in wait,
preying upon, informing against, and hanging one another: A Crowd
of Fools, Knaves, Whores, and Hypocrites." Yet Gay never puts things
quite so bluntly. Possibly (he suggests) the dominant passion is not interest but love, which finally conquers all: *"Can love be controul'd by advice?"* Polly sings; "How the mother is to be pitied who hath handsome
daughters!" Mrs. Peachum complains, "Locks, bolts, bars, and lectures
of morality are nothing to them: they break through them all." But then,
by gradual steps, Gay closes off that sentimental possibility. As Empson's
fine account of the play demonstrates, Polly's passionate love for Macheath is subtly presented as being as self-interested and destructive as
the tradesman's or the criminal's passion for financial advancement; the
tightening of the marriage knot can be as deadly as the tightening of
the hangman's. In her ardent quest for the sociability of marriage Polly
can look like a beast of prey.

To see how Gay gently subverts the sentimental Shaftesburian premiss about the benign workings of the human passions, we may explore
a little further the sources and implications of his literary parody in
the final scene of the play. The memories of *Venice Preserv'd* in this
scene I have already noted. Overlaying these, however, are other memories of another equally famous heroic tragedy. Polly and Lucy, standing
imploringly on either side of Macheath, may well (as earlier critics have
suggested) have put an audience in mind of Robert Walpole's wife and
mistress struggling for the great man's attention, or even conceivably
of Handel's two leading sopranos, Cuzzoni and Faustina, to whom the
beggar obliquely alludes in the play's introduction. Yet they would also
probably have reminded an audience of Dryden's Octavia and Cleopatra, competing in that famous scene in Act III of *All For Love* for the
affection of Antony.

Which way shall I turn me—how can I decide?
Wives, the day of our death, are as fond as a bride

is how Macheath expresses the struggle, echoing the words of Antony
before him: "O Dolabella, *which way shall I turn?"* Antony's struggle is
expressed in tears and blushes, the simple appearance of the two women
being sufficient to draw forth all his instinctive, though conflicting, affections of pity, shame, and love: the scene might be described as heroic-
sentimental. Macheath's struggle is very different:

One wife is too much for most husbands to hear,
But two at a time there's no mortal can bear.

Macheath's dilemma is a dry and intellectual one: how do I get out of this fix? In *Spectator* 44—the same number in which he had mocked the stage device of tolling bells—Addison examined other "Artifices to fill the Minds of an Audience with Terrour" which were then in popular use, and descended with patricular and merciless wit upon this very scene in *All For Love*. Dryden's Octavia, it will be remembered, makes her entrance in this scene *"leading* ANTONY's *two little daughters."* A disconsolate mother with a child in her hand, Addison remarks, is a convenient device to draw compassion from an audience. "A Modern Writer," he goes on, observing the fact and "being resolved to double the Distress," introduced a princess on stage leading a couple of children by the hand; this was such a success that a third writer, not to be outdone, resolved to introduce three children, thus scoring an even greater triumph; and, says Addison, that is not all:

> . . . as I am inform'd, a young Gentleman who is fully determin'd to break the most obdurate Hearts, has a Tragedy by him, where the first Person that appears upon the Stage, is an afflicted Widow in her Mourning-Weeds, with half a Dozen fatherless children attending her, like those that usually hang about the Figure of Charity. Thus several Incidents that are beautiful in a good Writer, become ridiculous by falling into the Hands of a bad one.

With the sudden production at the end of *The Beggar's Opera* of four more wives for Macheath—making six in all on stage—all four bearing "a child a-piece," Gay clinches the same comic point that Addison had made in *The Spectator*. The fallacy which Gay's parody implicitly attacks is not simply that of believing that pathos can be increased mechanically, like troops in a stage-army; it is also the sentimental fallacy of believing that the mere presence of wives and children will reduce us, mechanically, to tears and hugs and blushes. The affections do not operate with quite the happy regularity which Dryden and Shaftesbury, in their different ways, had suggested. There are times when one would rather stick one's head in the hangman's noose than be sociable any longer.

The final escape-route can only be to death, but that "the taste of the town" will not allow, and Macheath is saved by a reprieve. The last and cruellest irony is that the sentimental passions will not only drive a man to drink and to the gallows, but that they will also rescue him from those final avenues of freedom with an ominous promise of the nuptial bliss which awaits him:

> But think of this maxim, and put off your sorrow,
> The wretch of to-day, may be happy to-morrow.

It is characteristic that the play should close upon such an ambiguous promise of happy days.

Gay's ironical concession to "the taste of the town" at the end of *The*

Beggar's Opera reminded Colley Cibber of Jonson's similar ironical con-cessiveness in *Bartholomew Fair*,[23] and on this point, as on other points, the two plays are indeed alike. Each uses similar methods of comic level-ling and inversion, bringing before us the fact that, despite all evidence to the contrary, all men are alike; were it not for the reprieve, says Gay's Beggar regretfully, his play would have carried a most excellent moral, "that the lower sort of people have their vices in a degree as well as the rich: And that they are punish'd for them." Both plays operate on a double level, entertaining their audiences so agreeably that their ironical undercurrents are not always fully discernible. Both plays move genially to their conclusions, with a wry knowledge of the way in which the theatrical public will like events to be resolved. Both plays—but most of all, *The Beggar's Opera*—maintain to the end an element of tease, of take-it-which-way-you-will. In its various and seemingly contradictory ways, for its pathos and its bathos, as a sentimental lollipop and as a terse social fable, *The Beggar's Opera* will no doubt continue to give equal delight. To deceive us so variously and so well is a triumph of the counterfeiter's art.

[23] *An Apology for the Life of Mr. Colley Cibber*, ed. Robert W. Lowe (London, 1889), i. 245.

From *The Beggar's Opera*

by Bertrand Harris Bronson

. . . Gay has invented for us a vivid group of people, with an appeal that is hard to resist. They are so delightful, and, in the discrepancy between their reprehensible ends and the self-righteousness with which they pursue them, so ludicrous that we may miss the richer significance of the satire in our mere spontaneous enjoyment. The matter is treated with so light a hand that we incline to ignore its serious implications. It is important, therefore, to remind ourselves of the actual weight of these persons, for without this solid underpinning Gay could hardly have made his play carry the considerable cargo of its deeper meaning

"*From* The Beggar's Opera," *by Bertrand Harris Bronson. This selection is from* Facets of the Enlightenment: Studies in English Literature and Its Contexts, *by Bertrand Harris Bronson. (Berkeley and Los Angeles: University of California Press, 1968), pp. 81–90. Originally published by the University of California Press; reprinted by per-mission of The Regents of the University of California. This essay first appeared in* Studies in the Comic, University of California Publications in English, 8 *(1941), pp. 197–231.*

—could hardly have made it a social commentary which, for all its surface playfulness, fulfills some of the profoundest ends of comedy.

Each of the leading characters is a positive force. Let us hold in abeyance for the moment our amused perception of their real worth, while they parade before us in the favoring light of their own self-regard. Peachum is a man of responsibility who has constantly to make decisions affecting the welfare and the lives of many people. He has to weigh the importance of particular cases, adjudicate conflicting claims, and issue commands. And his orders are not lightly disobeyed. His wife has a proper sense of her husband's importance in their world, and of her own position. She shares his counsels, but respects his authority and does not abuse her privilege. Her solicitude for her family's reputation is keen, her maternal sense is well developed. She does not lightly give way to emotion, but, on a sufficient occasion, her passions are impressive. Polly is neither feather-brained nor impulsive, but basically prudent and steady. She accepts, and respects, her parents' values, and her single point of difference with them is rationally grounded though admittedly in significant accord with her inclinations. Filch, the servant, recognizes that his own interests are identified with his masters', and is accordingly trusted and accepted almost as one of the family. He is a boy of the brightest parts, quick and apt, ready to give his best efforts to the discharge of his varied responsibilities. Lockit is another, but lesser, Peachum, with a philosophy equally well developed though not quite so fully uttered, and with a visible satisfaction in the power he wields. His daughter Lucy is a Salvator Rosa set over against the Claude of Polly. In her tempestuous nature we can trace Ercles' vein:

> The raging rocks
> And shivering shocks
> Shall break the locks
>   Of prison gates.

She has a streak of tenderness, but in anger she is terrible and dangerous. She is crafty and determined in pursuit of revenge, and does not flinch from the possible consequences. As for Macheath, his sang-froid, dash, and prodigality of purse and person make him a favorite with both sexes. He is not easily cast down, and he knows that there are things worse than death in the human lot. Hazlitt calls him "one of God Almighty's gentlemen." His gallantry and good breeding rise, declares Hazlitt, "from impulse, not from rule; not from the trammels of education, but from a soul generous, courageous, good-natured, aspiring, amorous. The class of the character is very difficult to hit. It is something between gusto and slang, like port-wine and brandy mixed." [1]

None of these persons appears to be suffering from a sense of in-

[1] *On the English Stage,* July 27, 1816, quoted by W. E. Schultz, *Gay's Beggar's Opera: Its Contents, History and Influence* (1923), p. 274.

feriority. Their words give proper dignity to their ideas, and their conduct proceeds in accordance with principles to which they have given a good deal of thought. Without in the least minimizing the pleasure of their company, one may assert that, with the possible exception of Polly, they all have a better opinion of themselves than we do. For we are not taken in: we know them for the immoral rogues that they are. They are the most immediate objects of Gay's satire. However loftily they bear themselves, the human reality of their lives is sordid and contemptible. Remembering the dreariness of many of the products of "realism" in later days, we may well be grateful for an occasional example of the mock heroic, which subjects to the purposes of humor the matter generally reserved for "realistic" treatment. The flair for this inverted kind of burlesque has, for reasons which might elsewhere be significantly pursued, been all but lost in our time. It is enough to note here that, in our recognition of Gay's burlesquing of the high-flown manners and sentiments of operatic romance, we ought not to lose sight of the fact that he is simultaneously ridiculing a low society by decking them in all this borrowed finery. For burlesque has a two-edged blade, though both edges need not be equally sharp. "Had the Play remain'd, as I at first intended," says Gay in the person of the Beggar, with glancing irony, "it would have carried a most excellent Moral. 'Twould have shown that the lower Sort of People have their Vices in a degree as well as the Rich: And that they are punish'd for them."

The characters in the play are aware of our low opinion of them, and stand on the defensive against us. Offspring of corruption as they are, feeding on sin and death, what are their bulwarks, that so magnificently shore up their self-respect?

It is not by maintaining that the bases of our criticism are unsound that they are able to repel our attack. Truth and falsehood, good and evil, right and wrong are for them fundamentally the same as they are for us. Peachum, for example, accepts the conventional morality, and can even afford to make gestures of kindliness when they do not interfere with more important considerations. He delights "to let Women scape." "Make haste to *Newgate*, Boy," he commands Filch, "and let my Friends know what I intend; for I love to make them easy one way or other." And Filch, in the orotund fashion of sentimental drama, replies, "I'll away, for 'tis a Pleasure to be the Messenger of Comfort to Friends in Affliction." Neither Filch nor Mrs. Peachum is a stranger to feelings of gratitude and good will. Peachum, moreover, is above petty animosities. When Polly recoils from the idea of having Macheath impeached, protesting that her blood freezes at the thought of murdering her husband, Peachum replies:

> Fye, *Polly!* What hath Murder to do in the Affair? Since the thing sooner or later must happen, I dare say, the Captain himself would like that we should get the Reward for his Death sooner than a Stranger. Why, *Polly,*

the Captain knows, that as 'tis his Employment to rob, so 'tis ours to take Robbers, every Man in his Business. So that there is no Malice in the Case.

Clearly, these are no devils. Evil is not their good.

Rather, they stand us off by admitting the justice of our cause and then diverting our attack all along the line to their betters. Gay himself is easily deflected and we follow him in full cry. Here we reach the second degree of his satire, and it is on this level that the main attack is launched. People in the honorable walks of life—men of great business, ladies of fashion, lawyers, courtiers, statesmen—it is these who come in for the hottest fire. "Murder," declares Peachum, "is as fashionable a Crime as a Man can be guilty of. . . . No Gentleman is ever look'd upon the worse for killing a Man in his own Defence." If Macheath cannot do well at the gaming tables, the fault lies in his education: "The Man that proposes to get Money by Play should have the Education of a fine Gentleman, and be train'd up to it from his Youth." "Really," replies Mrs. Peachum to her husband, "I am sorry upon *Polly's* Account the Captain hath not more Discretion. What business hath he to keep Company with Lords and Gentlemen? he should leave them to prey upon one another." Society is a casino. Both sexes play; and since the only purpose that motivates their play is the desire of gain, it follows that very few persons are above sharp practice. "Most Ladies take a delight in cheating, when they can do it with Safety," declares Mrs. Trapes. Gamesters are the vilest of Mechanics, but "many of the Quality are of the Profession," and they have admittance to the politest circles. "I wonder," remarks Matt of the Mint, "I wonder *we* are not more respected."

> Thus Gamesters united in Friendship are found,
> Though they know that their Industry all is a Cheat;
> They flock to their Prey at the Dice-Box's Sound,
> And join to promote one another's Deceit.
> But if by mishap
> They fail of a Chap,
> To keep in their Hands, they each other entrap.
> Like Pikes, lank with Hunger, who miss of their Ends,
> They bite their Companions, and prey on their Friends.

Money will do anything in this fashionable world. Ladies marry in hopes of soon being widows with a jointure. When Polly announces that she has married for love, her mother is horrified: "Love him! I thought the Girl had been better bred." And to marry a highwayman: "Why, thou foolish Jade, thou wilt be as ill us'd, and as much neglected, as if thou hadst married a Lord!" But Polly herself knows—at least in her own opinion—"as well as any of the fine Ladies how to make the most of my self and of my Man too."

No love is lost in those exalted spheres. And even friendship proceeds merely upon the foot of interest. "Those that act otherwise are their own Bubbles." Promises are plentiful, but a court friend was never known to give anything else. Quite the contrary: "In one respect," says Peachum, "our Employment may be reckon'd dishonest, because, like great Statesmen, we encourage those who betray their Friends." But again: "Can it be expected that we should hang our Acquaintance for nothing, when our Betters will hardly save theirs without being paid for it?" And think of the legal profession. Robbery may be common elsewhere, but beside the wholesale robbery of the law it is nothing at all. "Gold from Law can take out the Sting," but, on the other side,

> It ever was decreed, Sir,
> If Lawyer's Hand is fee'd, Sir,
> He steals your whole Estate.

It appears, then, that if the Newgate people are culpable, they are merely imitating their betters, who must be charged with equal blame. But grant so much, and we must grant more. The criminals press their advantage by suggesting that guilt is proportional to the amount of harm done, which in turn depends on the degree of power to execute it. There is no question where the power resides. The statesman may think his "trade" as honest as Peachum's, but logic will say him no. Thinking of our own days, we shall have little heart to contradict logic. Then, sings Macheath unanswerably:

> Since Laws were made for ev'ry Degree,
> To curb Vice in others, as well as me,
> I wonder we hadn't better Company,
>   Upon *Tyburn* Tree!

> But Gold from Law can take out the Sting;
> And if rich Men like us were to swing,
> 'Twould thin the Land, such Numbers to string
>   Upon *Tyburn* Tree!

Moreover, Macheath and his gang have one more shaft to shoot, for what it is worth. They can set an example of loyalty and generosity and honor among themselves. "Who is there here," cries Nimming Ned, "that would not dye for his Friend?" "Who is there here," adds Harry Padington, "that would betray him for his Interest?" "Show me a Gang of Courtiers," says Matt of the Mint, "that can say as much." Macheath prides himself upon being a man of his word and no court friend. "We, Gentlemen," he declares, "have still Honour enough to break through the Corruptions of the World.—And while I can serve you, you may command me."

Here the defense rests its case. The ground has been occupied before,

and will be again. The abuse of power, the chasm between profession
and practice in high place, the constant defeat of principles by wealth,
the oppression of desert born a beggar, "the spurns that patient merit
of the unworthy takes," the immorality and selfishness of privileged
society—all these themes are the stock-in-trade of satirists, familiar to our
ears as household words. This is the habitual level of Swift, whose way
is to show how much more reprehensible those are whom the world
admires than those whom the world despises.

But Gay's satire does not stop at this point. There are hints in *The
Beggar's Opera* of a more revolutionary doctrine. If we really believe in
truth and justice and the general welfare, doubtless we should all be
glad to see temporary violations of these principles set right. We should
welcome, should we not, a fairer distribution of this world's goods, juster
apportionment of the right to life, liberty, and the pursuit of happiness?
But do we not, on the contrary, resist by all the means in our power
any attempts at readjustment? Are not Macheath and his fellows more
active laborers for the general good than we? We adopt the principles
but obstruct their realization. The Newgate gentry adopt them and work
for the cause:

> *Ben Budge.* We are for a just Partition of the World, for every Man hath a
> Right to enjoy Life.
> *Matt of the Mint.* We retrench the Superfluities of Mankind. The World is
> avaritious, and I hate Avarice. A covetous fellow, like a Jack-daw, steals
> what he was never made to enjoy, for the sake of hiding it. These are the
> Robbers of Mankind, for Money was made for the Free-hearted and
> Generous.

Who, then, are the true friends of man? Are they not the so-called
enemies of society? Is it possible to be actively a friend of mankind without being a revolutionary? The established order is radically iniquitous:
how can we defend the *status quo* and remain true to the principles to
which we profess allegiance?

Thus it becomes clear that *The Beggar's Opera,* half a century before
Figaro burst upon the world, foreshadowed in significant ways the point
of view which Beaumarchais was to develop with such devastating results.[2] That the political and social implications of the earlier work did
not explode with equal violence is in large measure due, of course, to
the different temper of society at the time. But equally it is due to the

2 "Mais il y a un jour où se remassent dans une explosion unique tous les sentiments
de toute nature, moraux, politique, sociaux, que l'oeuvre des philosophes avait
développés dans les coeurs, joie de vivre, avidité de jouir, intense excitation de l'intelligence, hains et mépris du présent, des abus, des traditions, espoir et besoin d'*autre
chose:* ce jour de folie intellectuelle où toute la société de l'ancien régime applaudit
aux idées dont elle va périr, c'est la première représentation du *Mariage de Figaro* (27
avril 1784)."—Lanson, *Hist. de la Litt. Française,* p. 807.

broader base of Gay's satire. Figaro, besides being the spokesman of democratic defiance against rank and privilege, is basically the wholesome representative of those conventional virtues that popular sentiment judged worthy of perpetuation. He is therefore a revolutionary symbol to which generous souls could pay sympathetic homage.

There is no comparable figure in the earlier play. For the Newgate knaves, however they may color their actions, are only masquerading. When their conduct is scrutinized, it is obvious that self-interest is at the bottom of everything they do. It is shot through with bad faith and disloyalty even to their own class. Jealousy and suspicion are the rule here as elsewhere. In the end, Macheath is forced to draw the inevitable conclusion from his experience: "That *Jemmy Twitcher* should peach me, I own surpriz'd me!—'Tis a plain Proof that the World is all alike, and that even our Gang can no more trust one another than other People."

The world is all alike! That is the final lesson of Gay's satire. We laughed at the obvious reversal of accepted values which runs through the play. We laughed to hear Black Moll's industry commended, knowing that that industry was actively expended upon thievery and playing the whore. Laziness is a vice, and it was refreshing to see sloth in the performance of crime meet with its due punishment. But, *mutatis mutandis,* were we not laughing at ourselves? As Peachum told his wife, "The World, my Dear, hath not such a Contempt for Roguery as you imagine." We are all cheats, paying lip service to one set of principles and motivated in actual truth by another. Every man presents to the world an idealized dream picture as his authentic and veracious self-portrait. The institutions of society, which we pretend are so solidly established, rest on a fiction that has no external actuality. The ideals we profess are impossible to live by in this world, for they are undermined both from within and without. Private interest seldom coincides with public good, and private interest has the controlling hand, whether in the political, the social, the commercial, or the sexual sphere. Of this truth we are reminded in the play. "Now, *Peachum,*" soliloquizes Lockit, "you and I, like honest Tradesmen, are to have a fair Tryal which of us two can overreach the other." "All men," reflects Mrs. Peachum, "are thieves in love, and like a woman the better for being another's property." "Of all Animals of Prey," says Lockit, again, "Man is the only sociable one. Every one of us preys upon his Neighbour, and yet we herd together." "Well, Polly," sighs Mrs. Peachum, "as far as one Woman can forgive another, I forgive thee." The opposition of class against class, youth against age, sex against sex, individual against individual, is both inevitable and involuntary. We are predatory by the mere physiological premisses of our common humanity. Under the conditions of existence, idealism is a merely relative term. "Oh, gentlemen," cried Hotspur before he died,

> the time of life is short;
> To spend that shortness basely were too long
> If life did ride upon a dial's point,
> Still ending at the arrival of an hour.

The irony is that, paying homage all our lives to these principles, it would hardly be possible to point to a single hour in which we lived in entire accordance with them. This is the doom of man, and each of us postures as if it were reversed for him, condemning others for what he excuses in himself, and generally playing such fantastic tricks before high heaven as are enough to make immortals laugh themselves to death. Fixed in this dance of plastic circumstance, we persist in declaring that we are the captains of our souls. Existence itself is the ultimate irony.

To go on breathing in the utter vacuum of this realization is impossible, and most of us are able to enter it only at rare moments. Acceptance of the pessimistic view may generate reactions which are diametrical opposites. The picture may be seen as comedy, or it may be seen as tragedy. To the romantic vision, speaking generally, it will appear tragic; to the classical, comic. The romantic attitude, being chiefly concerned with the individual ego, finds this spectacle of a divided self all but intolerable, and, to restore inner consistency, may take refuge in the Byronic pose. If I cannot be true to the ideals I profess, let me overturn those ideals and set up others that will be valid, and in accordance with the facts of my existence. "Evil, be thou my good!" Thus, in solitary grandeur, the diabolist may enjoy the luxury of integrity. For man in society, however, such an escape is hardly possible. The eighteenth century was not an age of solitaries; its characteristic orientations concerned man as a social being. It took little pleasure in exploring the orbit of the lonely soul through infinite space; it derived strength and assurance from solidarity. The contradictions of life become once again endurable when shared with one's brother men, and it is possible to be objective in contemplating the universal lot. Thus the age of Gay tended to see the irony of existence as fundamentally comic. For Swift, indeed, who had to watch the comedy through eighteenth-century eyes but with the passionate emotions and gigantic ego of a romantic, the spectacle turned bitter. Gay's good-humored view of it, as seen in *The Beggar's Opera,* is essentially characteristic both of his age and of himself. It was Gay who devised for his own epitaph the well-known lines:

> Life is a jest; and all things show it.
> I thought so once; but now I know it.

Chronology of Important Dates

	John Gay	The Age
1685	Gay born in Barnstaple, Devon.	Death of Charles II; accession of James II.
1688		The Glorious Revolution (William and Mary).
1695		Death of Henry Purcell.
1701		War of the Spanish Succession.
1702	Apprentice to a mercer, London.	Accession of Queen Anne.
1707	Secretary to Aaron Hill.	
1708	*Wine,* his first poem published.	
ca. 1711	Begins friendship with Pope.	
1711		Handel arrives in England; his *Rinaldo* written and performed.
1713	"Scriblerus Club" formed.	Treaty of Utrecht ends the War of the Spanish Succession.
1714	*The Shepherd's Week;* secretary to Lord Clarendon on a diplomatic mission to the Court at Hanover; "An Epistle to a Lady Occasion'd by the Arrival of Her Royal Highness."	Death of Queen Anne; accession of George I.
1715	*The What D'Ye Call It* (containing the ballad " 'Twas when the seas were roaring," which was set to music by Handel).	"James III," the Pretender, attempts unsuccessful invasion.
1716	*Trivia; or, the Art of Walking the Streets of London.*	
1718		Statute against Jonathan Wild's scheme.
1719	*Acis and Galatea,* set to music by Handel, performed privately at Cannons, the estate of the Duke of Chandos.	The Royal Academy of Music formed to support an Italian opera company.
ca. 1720	"Sweet William's Farewell to Black-ey'd Susan" (the ballad be-	

ginning "All in the Downs"); it was set to music by Carey, Leveridge, Haydon, and Sandoni.

1720   *Poems on Several Occasions;* Gay invests and loses his large profit from the *Poems* in the South Sea Bubble.

1721   Robert Walpole becomes First Minister.

1723   Becomes Commissioner of State Lotteries; reads his play *The Captives* to the Princess of Wales.

1725   "Newgate's Garland: being A New Ballad shewing How Mr. Jonathan Wild's Throat was cut from Ear to Ear with a Penknife, by Mr. Blake, the bold Highwayman, as he stood at his Tryal in the Old-Bailey."   Jonathan Wild hanged.

1726   Long visit by Swift during the summer.   *Gulliver's Travels.*

1727   *Fables,* First Series (dedicated "To His Highness William, Duke of Cumberland"); Swift returns for another long visit in the summer, staying often with Pope and Gay at Twickenham; Gay offered the post of Gentleman Usher to the Princess Louisa, which he refuses.   Faustina and Cuzzoni quarrel onstage at the Opera; death of George I; accession of George II.

1728   *The Beggar's Opera* opens January 29 at Lincoln's Inn Fields; its sequel, *Polly,* refused license for performance.   *The Dunciad.*

1729   *Polly* published by subscription; Gay loses his apartments at Whitehall; goes to live with the Duke and Duchess of Queensberry.

1732   Gay dies December 4; buried in Westminster Abbey.

1737   The Stage Licensing Act.

Notes on the Editor and Contributors

YVONNE NOBLE, the editor of this volume, has recently left an associate professorship at the University of Illinois at Urbana-Champaign to live with her husband and children in England. Her edition of *The Beggar's Opera* will soon be published, and she is now at work on a study of the imaginative influence of *Paradise Lost* on the masterworks of the eighteenth century.

BERTRAND HARRIS BRONSON is Professor Emeritus of English at the University of California at Berkeley. He is the author of books and articles on literature and folk music, including *Johnson Agonistes* and *In Search of Chaucer*, and is the compiler and editor of *The Traditional Tunes of the Child Ballads*.

IAN DONALDSON is Professor of English Literature at the Australian National University, Canberra. From 1962 to 1969 he was Fellow and Lecturer in English at Wadham College, Oxford, and from 1965 to 1969 an editor of *Essays in Criticism*.

WILLIAM EMPSON was Professor of English Literature at Sheffield University until his retirement. He has written many essays and poems as well as important and provocative full-length studies in literary criticism *Seven Types of Ambiguity* (1931), *Some Versions of Pastoral* (1935), *The Structure of Complex Words* (1951), and *Milton's God* (1961).

ROGER FISKE spent twenty years on the staff of the BBC and is now General Editor of the Eulenburg Miniature Scores. He has just published a full-scale history of *English Theatre Music in the Eighteenth Century*.

ERIC KURTZ has taught at the University of Wisconsin, Mount Holyoke, Wellesley, and Boston College, and is at present Dean of the Class of 1978 at Wellesley.

JOHN LOFTIS is Professor of English at Stanford University. He has written and edited numerous books on the Restoration and eighteenth-century theater and its public in London. He is General Editor of the Regents Restoration Drama Series.

MAYNARD MACK, Series Editor of *Twentieth Century Views* and *Twentieth Century Interpretations*, is Sterling Professor of English at Yale, former President of the Modern Language Association, and author and editor of many works on Shakespeare and Pope in their time and our own. He is at present at work on a biography of Pope.

HAROLD GENE MOSS is Assistant Professor of English at the University of Florida and Associate Director of the University's Center for Studies in the Humanities. He is author of essays on the ballad opera, eighteenth-century popular song, Fielding, and Gay.

MARTIN PRICE is Professor of English at Yale. He is the author of *To the Palace of Wisdom: Studies in Order and Energy from Dryden to Blake* and *Swift's Rhetorical Art: A Study in Structure and Meaning* and of essays on other aspects of eighteenth-century English literature and of the English novel.

Selected Bibliography

Editions and Recordings

The standard edition, *The Poetical Works of John Gay,* ed, G. C. Faber (London: Oxford University Press, Humphrey Milford, 1926), will soon be supplanted by John Gay, *Poetry and Prose,* ed. V. A. Dearing and C. E. Beckwith, announced to appear in the Oxford English Texts series.

Reliable editions of *The Beggar's Opera* that include its music are those in the Regents Restoration Drama series, ed. Edgar V. Roberts, music ed. Edward Smith (Lincoln: University of Nebraska Press, 1969), and in *British Dramatists from Dryden to Sheridan,* ed. George H. Nettleton and Arthur E. Case, 2nd ed. rev. George Winchester Stone, Jr. (Boston: Houghton Mifflin Company, 1969). Editions without music include two by contributors to this volume, one by Maynard Mack in *The Augustans* (Englewood Cliffs: Prentice-Hall, Inc., 1950 [English Masterpieces, Vol. 5]), and the other by Martin Price in *The Restoration and the Eighteenth Century* (New York: Oxford University Press, 1973 [The Oxford Anthology of English Literature, Vol. 3]), and an old-spelling text ed. Peter Elfed Lewis (Edinburgh: Oliver & Boyd, 1973). Yvonne Noble, editor of this volume, has nearly completed a scholarly edition that will include a realization of the score by Nicholas Temperley and reprinting of the words and music of the sources of the airs; this edition will be published by Princeton University Press. The historically most reliable edition of the vocal score is that ed. Edward J. Dent (London: Oxford University Press [1954]).

In recordings of *The Beggar's Opera* the music reflects later theatrical tradition rather than performance practice of Gay's own period. These include Frederic Austin's arrangement, conducted by Richard Austin (London A-4245); the Austin arrangement "orchestrated by Sir Malcolm Sargent" (Seraphim SIB-6023); and the only recording with all the airs, arranged by Max Goberman (Everest 6127/2 and 3127/2). In the film of *The Beggar's Opera,* 1953, with Laurence Olivier as Macheath, the music was arranged by Sir Arthur Bliss.

Biography and Correspondence

William Henry Irving, *John Gay: Favorite of the Wits* (Durham: Duke University Press, 1940) is the standard life of Gay.

The Letters of John Gay, ed. C. F. Burgess (Oxford: Clarendon Press, 1966) includes only Gay's side of his correspondence.

Selected Criticism

Arthur V. Berger, "The Beggar's Opera, the Burlesque, and Italian Opera," *Music and Letters, 17* (1936), 93–105, discusses aspects of Italian opera that became elements in Gay's burlesque.

Bertrand Harris Bronson, "The Beggar's Opera," *Studies in the Comic, University of California Publications in English, 8* (1941), 197–231, the last section of which is reprinted in this collection, also includes valuable discussion of Gay's sources in popular song and Italian opera.

William Empson, "Honest Man," Chapter 9 of *The Structure of Complex Words* (London: Chatto & Windus, 1951) includes discussion of the meanings of the expression "honest man" in *The Beggar's Opera*.

Roger Fiske, *English Theatre Music in the Eighteenth Century* (London: Oxford University Press, 1973), part of which is extracted in this collection, also offers the most informed treatment of how the music was handled in performance during the eighteenth century.

Edmond McAdoo Gagey, *Ballad Opera* (New York: Columbia University Press, 1937) offers discussion of possible sources for several aspects of *The Beggar's Opera* ("Low Life and the Musical Background"), a reliable summary of the first production and of the qualities that contributed to its exceptional popularity, and a detailed account of its successors in the genre.

Leo Hughes, *The Drama's Patrons: A Study of the Eighteenth-Century London Audience* (Austin and London: University of Texas Press, 1971), gives sound treatment to the debate over whether *The Beggar's Opera* was morally harmful, as well as to other aspects of its performance history in the eighteenth century.

William Eben Schultz, *Gay's Beggar's Opera* (New Haven: Yale University Press; London: Humphrey Milford, Oxford University Press, 1923) offers detailed and accurate information of all kinds on "Its Content, History, and Influence."

Patricia Meyer Spacks, *John Gay* (New York: Twayne Publishers, Inc., 1965 [Twayne's English Authors Series, Vol. 22]) is the best critical study of Gay's writing as a whole; Chapter 6, "The Beggar's Triumph," deals with *The Beggar's Opera*.